OUR STORIES IN PHILADELPHIA

*Joint Reflections on an 18-Year Urban
Immersion Program for Pre-service Teachers*

Edited by Julie Q. Bao, George R. Bieger and Larry A. Vold

Order this book online at www.trafford.com
or email orders@trafford.com

Most Trafford titles are also available at major online book retailers.

All royalty profits go to Larry Vold Urban Education Scholarship.

Printed in the United States of America.

ISBN: 978-1-4269-5122-0 (sc)
ISBN: 978-1-4269-5123-7 (hc)
ISBN: 978-1-4269-5124-4 (e)

Library of Congress Control Number: 2010918496

Trafford rev. 01/28/2011

 www.trafford.com

North America & international
toll-free: 1 888 232 4444 (USA & Canada)
phone: 250 383 6864 ♦ fax: 812 355 4082

Dedication

To all students and educators who are striving to advance urban learning conditions

Table of Contents

Editorial Board

Preface

How often in the teacher training programs of the United States do 500 pre-service teachers walk out of their comfort zones together to immerse themselves in urban settings to learn about different students and their special needs? How often in the history of American education does a state system of higher education continue sponsoring hundreds of their teacher candidates annually to inner cities for 18 years, and how often do professors from 21 universities converge in an urban environment and stay enthusiastically in student dorms to enhance learning of their students as well as their own?

These are some of the stories about the Philadelphia Urban Seminar. During the past 18 years, the Seminar facilitators have collaborated with hundreds of education administrators, thousands of cooperating teachers in over 60 inner-city schools and multiple community centers in Philadelphia. Moreover, the Urban Seminar has been supported consistently by a plethora of quantitative and qualitative data to attest to its strong impact on its participants. Consequently, the length, depth, scope, learning impact and its immersion feature of the Seminar have placed it among most effective urban teacher training programs for pre-service teachers in the United States.

Urban Education is one of the most challenging issues in American education today and has far reaching impact on American society in the twenty-first century. Yet, due to the complexity of the issue, demanding program logistics, cost of these immersion programs, and difficulty of obtaining authentic data in the field, very few books have been published pertaining to urban teacher training for pre-service teachers.

Therefore, the learning experiences that emanated from the Philadelphia Urban Seminar are worth sharing. The editors chose story-telling as the major mechanism to share these experiences because story telling is one of the most effective and time honored genres of literature. Stories told by dozens of participants from multiple perspectives can increase readers' comprehensive understanding of the urban conundrum. Moreover, it is the intention of the editors to use multiple personal stories to cancel out some of the idiosyncrasies and biases of individual participants, so as to present to the public a more balanced picture that may illustrate a cross section of the current conditions of urban teaching and learning.

In this book, each urban seminar participant tells an aspect of their personal experience. All stories are told with first person narrative except for a few introduction and research articles that provide program overviews and present research results. These poignant stories illustrate the soul searching impact of the Urban Seminar on pre-service teachers and demonstrate their excitement of learning in an urban setting. They also reveal frustrations of some urban school staff, admire efforts of cooperating teachers, highlight the need of social support for urban schools, and appeal to society and leadership for more profound changes in favor of urban learning environments. Many of these stories have made participants laugh, cry and think. In the process of developing their understanding of the inner-city intricacy, urban teaching dilemma, and circumstances of urban students, pre-service teachers also discovered their profound compassion, affirmed their aspirations, developed their teaching knowledge, skills and dispositions, and found their active roles in a participatory democracy.

At the end of each program, some teacher candidates choose to stay in the city with stronger sense of mission and commitment while others select to move on to other kinds of schools for various reasons. For those who decide to stay, they are better prepared to forge ahead in the urban environment; for those who decide to leave, they take with them a deeper human understanding to wherever they are teaching. As many participants commented that this profound urban immersion program would stay with them all their life.

This book is divided into six chapters. Chapter One provides an overview of the Philadelphia Urban Seminar. It introduces how the Urban Seminar has developed and its current operations. It also includes a faculty coordinator's flash back of seminar events, and a collective testimony of Shippensburg University's urban class of 2009. Chapter Two presents students' profound learning experience in inner-city schools. It ranges from unexpected encounters with urban students to in-depth reflections on a tough urban classroom; from initial shock and helplessness to compassion and tearful goodbyes. Learning the City of Brotherly Love is the theme of Chapter Three, which describes students' enlightening experience in the Philadelphia Art Museum, China Town, Historic District, community centers, as well as staying in the dorms of LaSalle University. Chapter Four highlights the choices of multiple Urban Seminar graduates to stay in urban schools, many of whom are currently teaching in inner-city schools of Philadelphia. Chapter Five selects research conducted by faculty and students, without which it is difficult to assess the effectiveness of the program. The final chapter emphasizes the collaborative efforts of faculty coordinators, school staff and community facilitators in making the program successful. In the closing article, the editors explain the current status of the program, use faculty testimony on the Urban Seminar to emphasize the importance of the urban education cause, and sum up the significance of the program. To protect privacy of students and people involved, all sensitive names of these stories have been changed.

The Philadelphia Urban Seminar was sponsored by Pennsylvania State System of Higher Education (PASSHE) in collaboration with the School District of Philadelphia. The editors want to thank all people and organizations that have made the Urban Seminar successful, which include the PASSHE Academy for the Profession of Teaching and Learning, the City and Regional School Districts of Philadelphia with their administrators, cooperating teachers and students, Norris Square and Germantown Community Centers, and all facilitators and pre-service teachers in participating universities. Additionally, we want to extend a special thank-you to authors that have contributed stories or research to this book. Faculty coordinators that edited their students' stories are serving on the Editorial Board of the book.

Finally, the editors hope that these stories will make more teachers, administrators and parents aware of the complexity of urban education issues, reflect on urban learning dilemmas, and appeal to more concerned citizens and decision makers for their greater support for urban students. After all, urban education is one of the most challenging issues in American education in the twenty-first century, upon which lies in the future of American cities, hence to a large extent, also the future of the entire country.

Editors

Chapter One

Introduction to Philadelphia Urban Seminar

The Philadelphia Urban Seminar has been in operation for eighteen years. Since its inception, thousands of pre-service teachers have participated in this innovative program. In this chapter, authors describe how the Urban Seminar began and how it continues to operate. Professor Larry Vold describes the origin and development of the Urban Seminar, and Professor Todd Hoover depicts how the program currently operates. The two weeks of learning and management are full of excitement and challenge which Professor Margot Vagliardo narrates as a faculty facilitator. Chapter one concludes with students' perspectives on the Seminar as summed up by Whitney Garner, writing for the Shippensburg University Urban Seminar Class of 2009.

Development of the Philadelphia Urban Seminar
Larry A. Vold

The year 2010 saw the 18th consecutive year of the Philadelphia Urban Seminar, which is an intensive and high impact inner-city immersion program for thousands of pre-service teachers facilitated jointly by educators of the District of Philadelphia, community partners as well as enthusiastic professors from 21 universities. Yet, the picture is very different from what existed twenty years ago.

By the early 1990s, the 14 Pennsylvania State System of Higher Education (PASSHE) Universities typically cooperated with public schools in their immediate geographic regions. Early field experiences and student teaching were done in the local public schools or at laboratory schools on the campus where the population was predominantly white with a rural or middle class background. Even those universities located in an urban area placed their pre-service teachers in suburban schools rather than schools in the inner city. There was a major disconnect between the types of communities for which we were preparing teachers and where the teaching jobs were actually located.

In the 1980s and 1990s Western Pennsylvania was witnessing an economic change of major proportions. The rapid loss of the economic base in the labor intensive industries of steel, coal, and related fields produced a major out migration that lowered the population. One effect was to reduce the need for hiring new teachers. Pre-service teachers graduating from PASSHE institutions in Western Pennsylvania were finding they could not be hired in their home towns or nearby areas. Jobs, however, were plentiful in new growth areas of the country and in urban areas, both of which were populated with high percentages of minority students with whom the new white teachers from the small towns and rural areas had little experience. Follow-up studies among the teachers indicated that some recent graduates were taking jobs in those areas but quickly became dissatisfied and looked to return to their home areas.

Program Development

At around this time, the Pennsylvania Academy for the Profession of Teaching and Learning (PAPTL), a part of the PASSHE, had begun to address the need for better preparing teachers for urban positions by first looking at the education professors in PASSHE schools. They quickly realized that the vast majority of professors had not been in a public school classroom in a long time and an even higher percentage had little experience in urban areas or in interacting with minorities. It seemed clear that professors could not teach what they did not know. So, a daring idea was developed and a new program was implemented: the Urban Scholars Program. The PAPTL asked the teacher education programs on each of the 14 campuses to identify at least two faculty members on each campus, who would be willing to meet as a group to read about and discuss urban education issues; commit to teaching in an urban public school for at least a couple of weeks; and initiate changes in their teacher education programs that would result in more attention to preparing teachers for urban schools.

A stipend was provided to all participants and, over a two-year period, there was a general increase in the discourse about urban education as these urban scholars returned to their universities and talked, some even excitedly, about their experiences in urban schools.

In 1991 a statewide conference was held in Philadelphia to share the experiences of the participants in the two cohorts of Urban Scholars. The following fall, at the annual Pennsylvania Association of Colleges for Teacher Education Conference, there was still a lot of excitement among the Urban Scholar members concerning their positive experiences in urban schools. A small group of student teacher supervisors, along with the director of the PAPTL and a few Urban Scholars, were sharing stories about their experiences in an urban environment. One of the topics that arose was the need for pre-service teachers to get experience in an urban setting prior to their student teaching experience. While the National Council for the Accreditation of Teacher Education (NCATE) and The Pennsylvania Department of Education standards called for a field experience in an urban setting or with a diverse population, the expectations were loosely interpreted and enforced. Almost any school district with several minority students was considered acceptable for providing the diversity experience.

The Urban Scholar student teaching supervisors made the point that only extensive prior contact and interaction with minorities would prepare the PASSHE students to be successful student teachers in an urban environment. They also raised the issue that there seemed to be little support on the respective campuses to develop those in depth types of experiences. Hearing the complaints, the Director of PAPTL offered a challenge to the group. She would provide seed money and some facilitating assistance if there were individuals who would develop a protocol model field experience that could be used by the various campuses. The challenge was accepted by nine professors from five of the campuses. With the support of the Director contact was made with the School District of Philadelphia which agreed to arrange visits to several of their schools across the K-12 levels. All of the schools chosen would be those with high minority populations and there would also be a mixture of schools that were academically solid as well as schools that were not meeting expectations and were considered hard to staff. In addition, the school district would arrange a series of meetings and discussions among the professors, central office administrators, regional superintendents, principals, and teachers. Those meetings would provide an opportunity for all parties to talk about the placement needs they had as well as concerns about the teacher education process. Meetings would also be held with several community agencies that dealt with a diverse population or offered cultural programs. For most of the professors the one-week experience provided a unique insight to a large urban school district and city environment. At the conclusion of the experience they returned to their campuses and shared with their respective deans what had transpired. Some loved it, others were less enthused, and some were turned off by the experience.

Nevertheless, there was uniform agreement, among the enthusiastic participants, that the school and classroom visits provided a real-world, hands-on environment that would benefit pre-service teachers. In the program that they envisioned, it was decided that the pre-service teachers would spend full days in the classroom for a two-week period. This extended time frame would provide a more realistic sense of what the teacher did during the day and also give some continuity to the teachers' on-going roles. This proposed approach was in sharp contrast to the model being used at the time, where students would find their own school placements and would go out on their own or in small groups for a couple of hours a day, once a week. The major objective in the existing model was to accumulate and document any hours in the field. By contrast, the new model would provide an experience where pre-service teachers could observe how race and culture impacted the teaching and learning process in the classroom and how the larger community related to the school.

Three of the original nine professors agreed to develop a similar urban field experience aimed at these goals for their pre-service teachers. With the support of their respective deans a recruitment strategy was designed and a special topics course was created to implement the experience. These three professors were from Indiana, Lock Haven, and Bloomsburg, which became the initial universities to pilot this urban field experience. These professors met several times during the fall semester to discuss recruiting strategies and other organizational issues. I agreed to explore what cultural groups or community agencies might be a better fit for our needs and which would also be willing to work with university pre-service teachers. I also agreed to serve as the liaison between the principals, regional administrators, and the universities.

The decision about which public schools to use was easy. Some principals and teachers thought that having university students for a couple of weeks would create more work for them and would be disruptive to learning. Other principals and teachers were enthusiastic and excited about the prospect. The choice of schools in which the pre-service teachers were to be placed would be very important and it was decided that the Region Five Area fit the bill. The Regional Superintendent was very supportive of the idea as were his central office staff and the principals in the region. In addition, the school population had a mixture of African American, Latino, Middle Eastern, and Asian students (Eligibility for Title One funds in these schools was typically above 90%), thus offering much greater diversity than was available in the districts traditionally served by the PASSHE universities.

Given that the university students were traveling a great distance from Western and Central Pennsylvania, transportation needed to be provided and housing needed to be available in relatively close proximity to the schools. LaSalle University met that criterion with dorm rooms being available. The professors would drive the students to their assigned schools, stay in the dorms with them, and structure meeting/reflection periods during which they could discuss how the students were processing their work in the schools.

The community component proved a bit more challenging. Activities were needed that would not interfere with the school day or the reflection and debriefing meetings after school. Since those were the more traditional academic components of the program they needed to be kept. Most community agencies had an after school program that conflicted with the planned university meetings and the professional development activities of the school district. One agency had Saturday programs and could also provide some interaction with parents. The decision was made to work with "The Norris Square Neighborhood Project" (NSNP). Sister Carol Keck, the Director, was flexible and willing to meet the universities' needs. The universities wanted pre-service teachers to meet parents and get a sense of the community, including an idea of what they thought about the schools. Beyond that, they were not sure what would be appropriate. It was left to them to decide what else they would like to do to help everyone better understand the community. That decision later turned out to be a critical and positive one. Community groups know what the problems were and what actions would help. They did not want "outside" agents coming in to tell them how to fix their problems.

Finally, the plans were in place, decisions had been made, and in May of 1993 twenty-six students and three professors began the initial trek to Philadelphia. The experience was successful beyond expectations. Students and professors had a variety of experiences from culture shock to better understanding. They witnessed excellent teaching and met remarkable, but economically poor and challenged students. They saw community people trying both to clean up a neighborhood and make it safe. Pictures taken by the students documented every new and exciting experience, and they felt welcomed in the schools and community. Phone calls home and discussions in the reflection meetings demonstrated that the impact of the experience on the pre-service teachers was significant. They felt a sense of pride and personal accomplishment because they had ventured outside of their secure home and university environments, they had learned a great deal, and they had not only survived but thrived.

From the very first experience it was the enthusiasm and excitement of the student participants that propelled the program forward. They talked with their friends about what they had learned and the personal growth that occurred through their close interactions with a variety of ethnic groups. They became more vocal in their education classes referring often to their real-world experience with minority students, much to the consternation of some professors who had not been in an urban classroom.

The second urban field experience was even better than the first. The professors were familiar with the city, the schools were happy to see them return and the NSNP expanded the students' involvement in the community by having students work in the community gardens and help with community clean-up, graffiti removal, and the clearing of vacant lots. Participants again viewed their experience positively and helped spread the word back on their campuses about this wonderful urban opportunity. Participant response to the urban field experience has remained positive from the very first trip to the last.

Program Expansion

There are organizational stages that any program experiences and the Philadelphia Urban Seminar was no exception. The first stage was the transition from a pilot program to an established program. Seed money designed to initiate any program ran out and the program needed to find a way to be self-sustaining. The bottom line for the program is that the students pay for the urban experience through tuition and other fees. To participate in the urban field experience, students paid tuition for the credits, they paid room and board costs for the two weeks in Philadelphia, and they paid a fee to cover miscellaneous costs such as the printing of program books, trips to cultural centers, speakers, etc. Those costs represent a substantial outlay of cash for the pre-service teachers.

From 1994 to 2003 there was a gradual growth in the number of participants on the three initial campuses. A fourth campus, Edinboro University, came on board in 1994 and Clarion University the following year. Expansion to Slippery Rock, California and West Liberty University in West Virginia occurred when Indiana's doctoral students who were involved with the Urban Seminar as part of their graduate program took teaching positions on those campuses. Another major impetus to growth came from the close personal involvement by faculty during the two weeks. These close personal interactions developed a sense of camaraderie and accomplishment among faculty members and promoted expansion to other campuses.

The growth of the Urban Seminar was greeted enthusiastically in the Central East Region of the Philadelphia School District. At the classroom level, teachers were happy to get an extra pair of hands in the classroom near the end of the year. The college students' enthusiasm was contagious. Administrators saw an increase in the number of student teachers and were later able to hire program graduates who, by then, had demonstrated their skills and established relationships with the schools.

The positive benefits of the program were that the universities began to identify outstanding mentor teachers and placed their students with them. Principals began to develop personal relationships and a sense of trust and credibility with the universities as well as an appreciation for the high quality of students that were being placed in the classrooms. Mentor teachers began to look forward to having high quality enthusiastic help in the classroom as well as student teachers who were there for a full semester. During the first five years of the program, the leadership in the Central East Region remained relatively stable and for the universities, there was no change in the professors who taught the course. This continuity in leadership early in the program was crucial.

In 2003, with the appointment of a Chief Academic Officer for the School District, an emphasis was placed on establishing partnerships with universities and outside agencies that would help the District meet its educational goals. The District would provide financial resources to support the partnerships. Outside agencies and universities could submit proposals to the School Reform Commission for consideration and funding.

The Pennsylvania Academy for the Preparation of Teaching and Learning had, over the years, increased its emphasis on involving PASSHE institutions in urban education, particularly in Philadelphia. A number of PASSHE institutions had individual programs or relationships with specific Philadelphia Schools and some indicated they would pursue a partnership grant. The Urban Seminar however, was the only cooperative program among several PASSHE institutions that worked in the Philadelphia School District.

The Director of the PAPTL met with me to explore the possibility of developing a partnership proposal with Philadelphia that would expand the Urban Seminar to all 14 PASSHE institutions. The idea of establishing a system-wide effort was powerful.

The partnership proposal to the School District was simple and straight forward. The PASSHE would develop, on a system-wide basis, an intensive field experience in the inner-city schools which would aim to change the negative perceptions of the School District and inner-city communities to a more positive perspective. They aimed to increase the number of Urban Seminar students and the number of student teachers placed in Philadelphia. The program provided funding to cover the food and lodging costs for the Urban Seminar students while they were in Philadelphia and a stipend to individuals if they came back to Philadelphia to student teach. It also provided for half of the cost of a full time program coordinator. The proposal was discussed with the non-participating PASSHE campuses and was enthusiastically accepted.

Faculty members were identified to teach the course and coordinate the program on each campus. Each year since the formal partnership began, student participation has grown. To accommodate the growth of university participants, more public schools were needed. The program moved into the North Region, East Region, and Central Region. The School District renewed the partnership and the program expanded to several more non-PASSHE universities and again the number of participants grew as the Northwest Region schools became part of the program.

In 2007 over 400 pre-service teachers were placed in 60 schools throughout the city. But circumstances change and, due to financial exigencies, the School District was no longer able to support the partnership financially. Because of the program's success in preparing teachers to deal with issues of diversity—and because of increasing growth in participating students and universities—the PASSHE assumed the operating costs.

Between 2007 and 2009 the Urban Seminar program continued to grow. In May of 2009 over 500 pre-service teachers were placed in nearly 70 schools in Philadelphia. They, along with 34 professors, came from 21 universities throughout the state. The rapid growth in participants from 2004-2009 was due, in part, to the state and school district funding. Another explanation for the growth is the high regard for the quality and impact of the program, as expressed by all the participants. Word of mouth on each of the campuses, by enthusiastic participants, made the program a prestigious and valued experience if one wanted to gain some knowledge and skills in urban environments. The program also has a tremendous impact on the personal development of each individual. Being submerged in the urban culture and community forced individuals to confront the stereotypes that they had heard all their lives. The experience produced a positive and powerful transformation, especially in students' attitudes and concerns about teaching in an urban setting.

While teacher preparation is not baseball, perhaps the maxim holds true, "If you build it, they will come." We have tried to build a better teacher education program and, indeed, they came. The last chapter of the Urban Seminar program has yet to be written but with 18 years of successful operations this program has demonstrated a compelling effectiveness.

(Larry A. Vold is a professor emeritus at Indiana University of PA.)

Site Operations of the Philadelphia Urban Seminar
Todd F. Hoover

What does a two week urban seminar really look like? What types of things will our students experience to actually help them as they pursue their goal of becoming an educator? Can two weeks really make a difference in the lives of the college students? These questions, and more, often run through the minds of students, university administrators, and the public in general, when they first hear about the Urban Seminar. Rest assured, the two weeks are filled to the brim with engaging, and often, life altering events that make the Philadelphia Urban Seminar an experience that our students comment on years after completing the program.

The experience begins with the arrival of students from all across the east coast as they converge on the City of Brotherly Love. Students spend the two weeks housed on the campus of LaSalle University. However, since we arrive on the Sunday following LaSalle's last day of the semester and clean-up is wrapping up, we are typically unable to go directly to the dorms upon arriving in Philadelphia. Therefore, the roughly 500 participants meet at a Philadelphia high school for orientation, van assignments, and other activities. As the program has built a highly positive reputation in the School District of Philadelphia, the superintendents from each of the regions volunteer their Sunday to meet with our students to give them an overview of their region's schools. More importantly, the superintendents share their gratitude for our students' willingness to help the school district's children and communities. Each superintendent typically gives our students a pep talk, and relates to the newcomers the many exciting things that are happening within their schools in an effort to supercharge them and welcome them as participants in the urban school's mission of improving the lives of its children and community.

The final part of the orientation is a group session, "Getting Your Mind Right," led by Urban Seminar veteran Professor Monte Tidwell. This is an opportunity for students to create the mindset needed to detail their goals for the experience, openly discuss their fears and expectations, and to begin to realize the difference this experience can have on the students they will teach over the next two weeks, and especially the impact it will have on themselves, both personally and professionally.

Following the orientation, the group moves to LaSalle University where the massive task of "move-in" takes place. Due to the finely crafted procedures developed over the years, what could be several hours of chaos typically goes rather smoothly with only a few minor bumps and glitches here and there. Within a couple of hours, the 500 new residents of LaSalle's dorms are in place and making themselves at home. After dinner, students typically meet with the professors from their home institutions in small group learning forums to review the syllabi, take care of any logistical issues, and to once again, reaffirm the significance of their roles.

Once the week begins, a typical day begins around 6:00 AM with showers and preparation for school. Vans, from the various universities sending the 500 college students, are lined up on the streets in front of the dorms. Students fill the vans around 7:30 AM and are transported to their schools where they spend the two weeks in the classroom. While at the schools, students have the opportunity to talk with faculty and staff about their experiences working and living in an urban setting, teach lessons, and carry-out many of the day to day tasks of a typical urban school teacher. The school day ends around 3:00 PM and most students return to LaSalle around 4:00 PM.

Figure 1.1 Go to school in the morning

On most days, there is a pre-dinner workshop scheduled from 4:00-5:15 PM. The workshops vary in nature. The first day is a Policies and Procedures presentation from our LaSalle Guest Coordinator. Other days include guest speakers, such as in 2009, Salome Thomas El, the man on which the movie "I Chose to Stay," and author of a book by the same title, is based. Salome's presentation discusses his life as a student growing up in Philadelphia, his years of post-secondary education, and his return to the city to teach and, eventually, become a principal. For several years, another presentation titled, "The Yellow Brick Road Syndrome: Teaching Urban Youth" has been offered by School District of Philadelphia's own Earl Carter. In it, Mr. Carter gives many real life examples of challenges faced in his career in urban education, leading to an inspirational message of hope. Another of the sessions is a New Teacher Panel, during which numerous first, second, and third year teachers from the school district share their thoughts and experiences about teaching in an urban school. To facilitate a more direct connection to the college students, this session is broken into two groups, one for elementary education majors, and another for secondary education majors. A new session for 2009, and one that sparked many lively discussions, was a presentation on the importance of a quality education both on the individual students, and on the city as a whole, by the mayor of Philadelphia, Michael Nutter. Finally, another example of a session held every year is the program led by the Human Resources Department of the School District. In it, students learn about the processes and procedures they can follow if they choose to student teach, and more importantly, begin their careers within the School District of Philadelphia.

Figure 1.2 Attending workshops after school

On many nights, dinner is offered in the Blue and Gold Cafeteria of LaSalle University. Students always comment positively on the quality of the food provided, in addition to the friendliness of the food services staff. Since the size of our group has grown so large, dinner is offered in two seating arrangements. In the off seating, students are encouraged to write in their daily journals, read the assigned readings, and work on their written course assignments. Of course, some of the students use the time to get in a quick cat nap as a result of the jam-packed schedule!

Following most dinners, the evenings have scheduled another small group learning forum where students meet to have class with their individual university instructors. These sessions involve many topics and activities, from "First Impressions" after the first day of school, to discussions of the events of the day, drawing connections between the assigned readings and what students are experiencing firsthand in the classrooms, and discussions of how this experience has impacted the students' pre-conceptions of teaching in an urban environment.

Over the years, there have typically been in-service days scheduled by the school district on one of the days during the time we are there. If the in-service day is one from which our students can benefit, they have been invited to attend these sessions. If the sessions are not directly connected to developing the skills of our students, then the Urban Seminar group has arranged alternate activities. For example, in 2009, many of the urban seminar coordinators offered a professional development conference the students were required to attend, with the following sample of topics: Teaching Urban Students of Color Using Multiple Intelligences; Simulations for Cross Cultural Awareness; Project Based Learning: Making the Curriculum Come Alive; Integration of Children's Literature into Culturally Responsive Lessons for Urban Students; Creative Insubordination: Teaching Subversively in Context of Standardization and Control; Domestic Violence and Its Effects on Student Learning; Conflict Resolution in Education; Developing Cultural Identities in the Classroom & the Impact on Teaching; Action Research For Teacher Candidates; A Conversation with Dale Mezzacappa, Contributing Editor of the Philadelphia

Public School Notebook; and Why Should Teachers Incorporate Community in the Classroom?

Another of the scheduled activities that takes place during the two weeks is an educational field trip to center city's historic district. Students attend a presentation at the National Constitution Center, have an opportunity to see the Liberty Bell and tour the Independence Hall, and learn about the educational programs available to teachers, as well as tour the Philadelphia Museum of Art, with internationally acclaimed work from Freda Kahlo to Frederick Remington to da Vinci and Monet.

Among highlights of the week for many students are the late evening educational field trips available to students. Through these activities, students get to experience the culture and life of the city; so that they can gain an appreciation of what opportunities are available to them should they decide to teach in an urban setting. These evening field trips include the Aspiring Jazz Musicians' Forum, a Philadelphia Phillies baseball game, visits to Old City or South Street, Salsa dancing lessons, or a stop at Pat's or Geno's (You can only be loyal to one!) for a Philly cheese steak.

The weekend between the two weeks is filled with activities as well. Saturday is devoted to community service, either near the Germantown Beacon Center or the Norris Square neighborhood. Projects involve trash clean up, painting park benches and railing, weeding and cultivating community gardens, designing and creating murals throughout the neighborhoods, and more. Each location serves the students a culturally significant lunch of "soul food" or Puerto Rican favorites. Following the meal, the afternoon is filled with a children's community festival at each location. Our students create activities and games to provide to the students and families of the community. This opportunity allows our students to see the children and their families in a different light and develops a bond between the community and the urban seminar that we each look forward to every year.

Figure 1.3 Visiting Norris Square Community Center

In this book, you will read about many of the experiences mentioned briefly in this overview. You will see, through the eyes and words of the participants, how these experiences affect them deeply. You will see how sometimes in the most surprising and unexpected moment, a person's life can be changed. You will see the true power of the Philadelphia Urban Seminar.

(Todd F. Hoover is an assistant professor at Bloomsburg University.)

Who Are the People Getting Off the Van?
—Reflections of an Urban Seminar Faculty Coordinator
Margot W. Vagliardo

Being a part of the Philadelphia Urban Seminar faculty is one of the most challenging, frustrating, stressful, exhausting, exciting, enjoyable, energizing, and rewarding two weeks I have ever experienced. The Seminar provides students (and faculty) with an "intense two week urban experience" (a phrase I insert into recommendations written for Seminar alumni) providing opportunities to connect with city children, teachers, schools, and communities. Experiences are purposefully planned to "facilitate students' appreciation and understanding of economic, social, cultural, racial and ethnic dynamics that impact the urban schools; practice culturally responsive teaching; and to better understand the concept of difference and their own ethnic, racial, and cultural identities" (University course syllabus, 2009), but often the most meaningful outcomes come from unplanned events. I am happy to say that the course goals have been met by the majority of students from my university who have attended. I am a white female professor who teaches about diversity and loves urban environments, and have been my university's coordinator and faculty-in-charge of students in the Philadelphia Urban Seminar for five years.

The following stories are some of the many that come to mind when I think back on Seminar experiences, whether intentionally designed or serendipitous, and how these events influenced the growth of my students and myself as we made meaning of our time in Philadelphia, and that brought me, as a teacher and mentor, closer to my students in ways not possible in a formal classroom situation. These stories include my voice and the voices of my students, taken from my notes and reflections, along with their journals and final papers. If you are or have been a faculty member or student in the Urban Seminar, I hope these reminiscences will also remind you of your own stories.

Who Are the People Boarding the Van to Go to Philadelphia?

Most of the students from my university who participate in the Philadelphia Urban Seminar are white middle class females[1]who have had few, if any, interactions with people who look and act differently than they and may have never been to Philadelphia or New York, even though our campus is within a two-hour drive of either city. These demographics mirror the total population of the university's College of Education. Most are from rural or suburban environments, often describing their hometown as "a place where there are more cows than people." Signing up for the Urban Seminar shows that they are ready to "try something different" and move out of their comfort zone with a two week immersion experience in an urban environment.

The air in the van is electric with energy, fear, and apprehension, and each year the students and I have these feelings as we leave our campus heading for Philadelphia. Who are these students stepping into the van, taking too many things in their attempt to be ready for anything? Usually the students do not know each other, and at this point are not aware that they share some necessary dispositions. They are adventurous and open minded enough to give up two weeks' summer work salaries and pay extra summer school tuition to commit to learning things they cannot foresee in an elective course called the Urban Seminar. One student, reflecting on her thoughts and fears before leaving for Philadelphia remarked: "based on dialogue with friends and family, I was convinced that I would be in constant danger while in the city" (after the Urban Seminar, this same student decided to student teach in the city and used public transportation to get to school in order to get "the true urban experience").

Where Are My Keys?

We arrive at the city school auditorium designated as the meeting point and are immediately joined by over 500 other students from more than a dozen other universities. It is usually somewhat

---

[1]   Of the 62 students who participated in the Urban Seminar, 57 are female. 1 student identified as Hispanic and 2 as African American.

chaotic, confusing, and hot. Faculty organizers have difficulty making themselves heard over faulty microphones. Having been warned to "chill out and be flexible," the students patiently wait to get schedules and the Seminar Reader, the course text; listen to introductions and short motivational speeches; and finally receive the all important van assignment, a universal source of worry, since this transportation is necessary to get to and from the assigned schools each day. The excitement is everywhere. One year, within ten minutes after reaching the designated school meeting place, a miscommunication resulted in the keys being locked inside our van. Thankfully, my AAA membership covered roadside service on the university vehicle! But I would wait outside for AAA and miss the orientation meeting. As luck would have it, the school district had forgotten to unlock the doors to the school, causing everyone to wait outside for an hour. Result: AAA unlocked the van, we all got into the meeting on time (albeit one hour late), and things progressed "normally."

Entering an Urban Culture

Stepping into a new culture, even for only a few weeks, can be challenging for anyone. For those who have grown up in other areas, preconceived ideas of "urban" reflects much of what the media portrays: noise, dirt, violence, and schools where children are not interested in learning, misbehave, teachers who do not care about and yell at their students, and parents who are not interested in their child's education. While some of these notions are unfortunately true, most are shattered by the personal relationships which form and quickly grow during the two week experience. Breaking down stereotypes and developing an understanding of urban issues and concepts of difference progresses throughout the two weeks as a major goal, and progress (or lack of) is revealed in student comments about the physical spaces, urban educators and learners, and urban "behavior."

Going for Groceries

Our first venture into city culture comes with the "grocery run" on the first night of arrival. The initial shopping trip is to a grocery store which serves the area in which we are staying is visually African American. This trip is, for many students, the first experience of being in the minority. Students shop with their new roommates and among people who look different than they. One student described the trip in journal entry:

As soon as I began walking to the entrance of the Shoprite, I noticed that I was in the minority. I could see everyone looking at me and I felt a slight tension. I am not used to being in situations like that. When I saw the man[2] dressed in black, I was instantly frightened. In my opinion, he looked like a terrorist. I know that this is incorrect and maybe it was a religious custom. However, his family (the people he was with), were not dressed like that. They had on similar clothes to the ones I had on. I made certain not to make eye contact with this person and quickly walked the other way. I have never been put in a situation where I am the minority and I felt like everyone was staring at me and I felt like they wanted me out of their town. I felt as if I could not ask anyone, including the employees, for any help finding an item because of the way we were watched.

Various shopping trips provided opportunities to make meaning of being a minority, a critical experience to have as one reflects on personal cultural identity. Situations as trivial as needing to buy beauty supplies can initiate small group dialogue and begin to derail the unexamined "default" White culture as the norm. "It took us awhile to find a plain hairbrush… Since all the stores carried mass amounts of waves and bristle brushes. Then we looked for brown mascara. All they had was black."

---

[2] The "man" was actually a woman wearing a *niqab*, a head scarf that reveals on the eyes.

Much of our nightly small group sessions focus on revisiting daily experiences and interweaving dynamic conceptions of race and culture, the complexity of cultural difference, and the danger of stereotyping.

Overlapping Roles

As a Seminar faculty member, my roles include being a teacher, mentor, manager, driver, and sometimes mom, to a dozen or so 18-25 year olds. I grapple with the same tenuous balance between allowing risk taking and being overprotective that I did with my own children, who are now in their 30's. I am the one who must manage and enforce our busy schedule of days in the schools, late afternoon professional development, assigned dinner times, small group meetings, and be cognizant of what people may be doing on their free time (of which there is very little). And, I am a driver. For the Seminar to work, one can not be afraid of driving or riding in a 12- or 15- passenger van in Philadelphia traffic. Faculty members and specially designated students transport participants to all seminar activities. We all soon learn about the Philadelphia driving culture—obsessive lane changes, running the red lights and jumping the green, and the middle lane parking on Broad Street. We become accustomed to trips being rerouted by "surprise" railroad tracks and no left turn signs, as well as managing oblique intersections and diagonal streets like Rising Sun and Germantown Avenue. We become skilled at negotiating neighborhood streets filled with excited children streaming from school doors. So, at least for some of us, ending our after dinner small group sessions with the necessity of swinging up into that driver's seat once again to pilot the van to South Street, Gino's Cheese steaks, Shoprite or Wal-Mart is not our first choice of activity. But every trip tests our commitment to urban experience and we go. One such venture comes to mind:

Birthday on South Street

OK, Alicia's twenty-first birthday is on Saturday during our two weeks of Seminar. Our all-female group wants to celebrate on South Street. They plan the outing, and let me know they will travel by subway; I do not have to drive. 'No,' I reply, 'there will be no riding the subway to Olney and walking the five blocks back to the dorm at night. Here is the deal: I will take you to South Street and you all take cabs back to the dorm or call me to come and pick you up, but you must call me before eleven-thirty.' Am I being unfair? Of course I know they are used to staying out later than that, but we are in the city, and I am responsible for them (Vagliardo, journal, 2007).

I get a call at 11:25PM, put my book down (I am at an exciting part, so I take it with me—who knows how long this will take) and drive our 15-passenger van to South Street at midnight. Where will I park this huge vehicle? I am annoyed. Thank God for cell phones. Luckily, one of the students has put herself in charge of getting everyone out on the street to wait so I can pull right up in front of the club. Karen is there, herding her very loud and "happy" classmates into the van. I am over my grumpiness, laugh at the students' stories of the birthday celebration, and praise them for their good decisions.

Learning about Urban Students and Urban Schools

I have observed similarities and differences in the ways in which students develop and expand their awareness, knowledge, understanding and confidence during and after their urban experience. Especially exciting is the role of a purposeful mediators (with course goals in mind) of the students' urban experiences, and that often the most meaningful experiences are those that are unplanned. The students' development is visible in daily debriefs and discussions, behaviors, journals, and the students' integrative papers; their final reflections on the urban experience submitted two weeks after their returning home. The visible impact ranges from a wider view of urban life and schooling to a life changing transformative experience.

Of course, a main focus of the Seminar experience is the time our students spend in an inner-city classroom. Working with a mentor teacher, students are provided varying levels of classroom experience, from working with individual students and small groups to being the de facto substitute for ten days. Our nightly small group meetings are a time of rich conversation. We meet together after dinner to discuss the events of the day, melding them with prior knowledge (and hopefully correcting mis-knowledge) as well as new facts, opinions, and issues that appear in the assigned articles in the Seminar Reader. The first small group meeting, after students have been in their assigned classroom for one day, is especially exciting. Students write down three adjectives that describe their school and/or classroom. Words range from: chaotic, shocking, appalling, noisy, needy, disrespectful, inappropriate, lazy, loud, energetic, to talkative and funny. Sharing the words creates a space in the group to discuss stories of day, reveal biases and stereotypes, and to examine the complexity of realities that prompted the choice of each descriptive word. Together, we make meaning of situations of which, before this day, many students had never witnessed.

The intensity of the two week Urban Seminar telescopes the process of getting to know the children in the urban classrooms, and participating pre-service teachers quickly form close relationships with many of their students. They are understandably upset when learning some details of their students' lives. Discussing urban realities provides opportunities to talk about default dominant White cultural standards and their relationship to measures of "normalcy." As students get to know more about the children in their classrooms, see the spark of wanting to learn in their eyes and they find numerous examples of what it means to be resilient, along with the critical role of the teacher in developing resilience in their students. Our discussions move toward transforming notions of the prevalent "at risk" thinking to that of "at promise," and connect with being active advocates for social justice. When is it right to deconstruct or to just empathize about an upsetting event in decision making? That is an ongoing decision for a faculty member of the Urban Seminar. Every day is replete with potential learning experiences.

Opening Eyes

"I learned something really important today," reported Janice during our small group meeting. Janice recounted a story that began two days before. She and her mentor teacher, a young, strikingly attractive African American woman, had been getting ready for her 27 kindergarten children to arrive for the day. Two teacher education students from a nearby university were also scheduled to spend some time observing. When the two (white) students entered the classroom, they proceeded to Janice to ask about their observation assignment. "I just said, 'oh no, I'm not the teacher' and directed them to Ms. T. Ms. T talked to them and they set up for the observation. I did not think anything of it." Janice then shared that the next day "Ms. T really seemed in a bad mood. We went to a faculty meeting and she turned to a colleague and complained about the way the two white university students had entered the room, and how she hated when that happened. "Then I got it," said Janice, "Those girls thought I was the teacher because I was white. I never, ever thought about that before!" Now we had another experience, unfortunately at the expense of a colleague, to think about and help us take another step toward a deeper understanding of racism and to finding our own ways to decrease it.

Snapshots of Urban Communities

Two weeks is certainly not enough time to get to know what urban life is about, and one must keep in mind that urban experiences can create or solidify stereotypes as easily as shattering them. To shine a light on the power and possibility of community actions in an urban neighborhood, weekend activities are planned to give the Seminar students a glimpse into urban communities. My students, along with others, travel downtown to Norris Square, a vibrant Puerto Rican neighborhood where the residents, through a long term commitment of working together, have revitalized the area by creating an urban garden and community center and keeping drug activity and related crime away. Students spend Saturday helping to clean up the local park and streets, participating in an afternoon festival for the neighborhood children, and are then treated to an authentic Puerto Rican dinner followed by Bomba dancing. The experience provides many opportunities to work with community members toward shared goals. What starts as a job of cleaning up "appalling" and "disgusting" streets and vacant lots becomes a deep respect for the power of collective action and shared culture. Students who have grown up on farms or in subdivisions get a close up look at city streets and sidewalks, row houses, vacant lots, and public playgrounds. Events like finding a dead animal in a plastic bag, an overgrown truck in an "urban jungle," cooling down in the water spraying from a fire hydrant opened by the police, being yelled at by a passerby who chastised the students for "cleaning up for people who do not do it for themselves," and eating a picnic lunch with local residents of various ages who are proud of their neighborhood help the Urban Seminar students understand the power of community.

Reflections on Community Events

My parental role was engaged when I noticed that two of the students were missing from the group assigned to clean up a block leading from the central neighborhood square. I was told that "Bill and Karen went in that house after a lady motioned for them to come in" by the remaining students who pointed to a shabby row house. "OK," I told myself, "I will just wait a little bit and they will come out." Maybe it was ten minutes, maybe it was twenty. It seemed like a long time, and I was getting ready to knock on the door when Bill and Karen came out. Breathing easier, I asked what they had been doing. Bill explained that

> While sweeping, Karen and I were asked (in Spanish) by an elderly woman to help her inside the house. She wanted us to fix her ceiling fan but it took awhile to understand what she was saying. Since I had taken three years of Spanish, I thought I would have been more capable. This was not the case; it took us about five minutes to figure out what she actually wanted. She was so grateful for our deed which made me feel great about myself. (Bill's journal)

What meanings were made from this situation? The importance of knowing another language? About people helping others and the positive feelings that come from an act of kindness? I reflected on my immediate fear for the students—did I invoke a stereotype of urban danger? Was my worry related to being a legally responsible faculty member? We had yet another real life scenario to discuss.

Sunday morning gives us all a second opportunity to experience different cultures through attendance at various church services. My students and I visited a Baptist Church in center city where all the parishioners are African American. The church's energizing service and gospel music is a new experience for most students. Not wanting to require attendance at a specific church, I initially made the trip a suggested activity. When the group debriefed the experience, the students unanimously agreed it should be mandatory. "The service was so exciting, and the members of the church were so welcoming to us. I have never been to a church like that before."

One very memorable visit occurred four years ago. As the church musicians were preparing setting up, Andrea, one of my students, noticed that the drummer, a young boy looking very smart in a little-too-large gold colored suit, was a student in the classroom to which she was assigned. He appeared very confident in his role, and for good reason; he was an excellent musician. Of course, the boy was thrilled to see Andrea, and we were able to take some pictures of the two of them before the service began. Later, in our discussion about the trip, I asked Andrea about how the boy did in school. "He is in trouble a lot," she answered, "he talks when he is not supposed to." Another wonderful "teachable moment," where personal experience bearing out what we know about schooling, children's "other lives," and success.

Who Are the People Returning to the University?

The final week of the Urban Seminar goes quickly. I keep a countdown of how many times more I have to make the twenty-five minute "van run" down Broad Street to deliver and pick up my students from their assigned school. My students and I have gotten to know each other. They are feeling more comfortable in their classrooms, continuing to get to know more about their students, and are talking like teachers. They need to take trips to Wal-Mart and the Dollar Store to buy small gifts for their students and mentor teacher. Several are making plans to come back to participate in class field trips and picnics. Stereotypes are falling away. Confidence is recognizable. Students are making meaning of the intense experience of which they have been a part. "Two weeks in this environment was completely out of my norm but sometimes we all need a life changing experience, I am starting to think this may be mine" (student journal reflection).

We go back to the descriptive adjectives during the last small group session. Students think hard before writing any words. Then they begin to share.

> *Disrespectful, frustrated, lazy* became *energetic, loving, and hard workers.*
> *Lazy, loud, disrespectful* became *funny, not understood, and full of energy.*
> *Unorganized, inappropriate, needy* became *respectful, crazy, and inspiring.*

The adjectives tend to reflect the realization of the complexity of an urban classroom. Students have numerous examples to illustrate the meaning of each word they have chosen. They have expanded their comfort zone, increased their confidence, and developed their understanding of culture and difference, including their own identity as a beginning educator and the identities of the students who will be in their future classrooms.

Who are the people getting back on the van to return to the university? They are teacher education students who now have a different understanding of urban learners, urban teachers, urban schools, and urban living. Everyone has had eye opening experiences, scary experiences, and joyful ones. Many students have indicated that the Urban Seminar was transformative; all agree it is an experience they will never forget. While not all participants go on to teach in urban schools, the demographic changes among families and students in the United States guarantee that beginning educators will face a diverse student population in their future classrooms. Whether or not they decide to teach in an urban school, all will go to their future classrooms more prepared and successful with all learners; those who look like them and those who do not. The Urban Seminar helps teacher candidates to develop the skills and attitudes needed in *all* classrooms as we strive to be culturally responsive educators who help to develop culturally responsive citizens. I am proud to have been part of the Philadelphia Urban Seminar.

(Margot W. Vagliardo is an associate professor at East Stroudsburg University.)

Testimony of Shippensburg University Urban Class of 2009
Whitney Garner

Barren playgrounds, limited textbooks, barred up gates surrounding the school grounds, colorless walls, students of mixed ethnicities, security guards, and stressed teachers. These were the types of ideas and impressions with which I was entering into the School District of Philadelphia. These were stereotypes that I had heard of from schools in my hometown and surrounding areas. These thoughts and images produce the stereotypes of inner-city schools, which are largely consequences of government's decades of neglect to the poorest downtown areas of the nation's metropolitan cities. In these settings gathered hundreds and thousands of children filled with diversity and desperately in need of large number of better trained and more committed teachers.

Coming from a small rural hometown surrounded with nothing but open fields and small housing developments the opportunity to experience an urban setting sounded incredible to me. I felt as though our education was not preparing us enough for the option of urban teaching, so I decided to try the Urban Seminar. Preparing at meetings at Shippensburg seemed so surreal in the beginning. It seemed as though we were planning for a journey which none of us were prepared for. Dr. Bao gave us information and background knowledge of her past experiences with the Urban Seminar and prompted us with questions and ideas for our trip. We went over things like what we would be doing there, and requested the grade level with which we would like to work, and when all was said and done we could do nothing but wait for our departure date.

Upon arriving in Philadelphia on May 17, 2009 we were overwhelmed with the idea of moving into the dorms at LaSalle University in Northern Philadelphia. We were given keys and roommate checklists and sent with our luggage to the dorms. As we approached, the building looked very old and seemed as though it had not been used for quite some time. Not having a choice, my roommate and I entered our room carefully taking in our surroundings. The dorms were relatively clean, but we soon found out that there were mice, and cockroaches on our floor, as well as a few of the other floors in the dorm. This was not a welcoming discovery, but we tried to keep in mind that we were there for the sole purpose of teaching and learning, not for a comfortable stay in a five star hotel. Distractions such as these could have caused us to get off task, but we chose as a group to remain focused on our goal in achieving an experience in an urban setting.

Our first meeting in Philadelphia for Urban Seminar 2009 was held at the High School down the street from La Salle University where we would be staying for the next two weeks. We entered the auditorium with over five hundred other students from universities all over Pennsylvania. There were some schools that brought close to one hundred students, some with twenty or thirty and there was our small fifteen passenger van group from Shippensburg. Even though we had a small group of students the individuals in our group possessed all the right attributes and eagerness to teach and to learn from this experience that enabled us to grow in our short time here. "I learned that teaching in an urban setting is very difficult yet very possible with the right mindset and attitude." (Muenker, 2009) The Urban Seminar program opened up doors for us that we may not have found on our own. "This was by far the most rewarding, hands-on, invaluable experience I have had in my life in a very long time." (Cromartie, 2009)

On the first day of going to my school, I had mixed emotions. I was nervous, excited, soft spoken (for once in my life), and just overall unsure of things. However, these feelings turned into pure joy after meeting with the school principal for the first time. We had a group meeting in the school library before we began our first day and were assigned to our classroom teachers. As the principal was going around telling everyone their placement she came to my name and my assignment. She turned to me and said "Oh boy, your class is quite a handful, but the teacher does a fantastic job." This statement remains clear in my mind to this day for one reason, because it made me so much more eager to get into the classroom. Challenges are exciting for me, and this seemed like the perfect opportunity to make a difference in some way.

The classroom I was assigned to was a fifth grade class under the supervision of a mid thirty-year-old African American woman who was fantastic. She had good control of the classroom, and the students really seemed to respect her as opposed to other teachers in the building. She informed me on the first day that most people do not realize that teachers in the city have more jobs than just being a "teacher." She informed me that she not only acts daily as a teacher but also as a parole officer, a babysitter, a doctor, a counselor, and everything else her students need her to be. This is why my respect started to grow for her on my very first day after that statement. I realized that she was not only there to teach, but to aid the students in whatever way they may need.

My classroom had twenty students, thirteen boys, and only seven girls. I had predominantly African American students with the exception of one Asian American and one Caucasian student. This allowed me to really experience diversity in the classroom and enabled me to expand my mind and really consider how to teach students with a different background than my own. "I learned that teaching in an urban setting requires a lot more emotional commitment than any other setting, some of the things that you will see and hear from your kids will shock you."(Leverentz, 2009) We were faced with instances in the classroom involving AIDS, brutal fights, severe language, sexual innuendos, and many other circumstances that should not be seen in an elementary school.

My placement ended up being a fantastic one, where I learned so much about inner-city schools, the children, home lives of students, teaching practices to reach students in urban settings, and much more. As I read my reflections over and over, I could only linger on a few thoughts and feelings that I had during my experience. Ones which made me realize that I am really cut out for this type of scenario. I realized that these students need committed teachers more than any other students. They come to school looking for love, attention, an education, a social life off the streets, a "family" like atmosphere, and acceptance overall. These students are faced everyday with the hardships of having to grow up way too quickly. Many of the students see fights and violence in general and feel as though they need to act out in order to gain attention, or in order to prove something to their classmates.

Fights were something that occurred frequently in my school. Our school was not protected by a security system at all. I found this interesting because all of my other group members talked about metal detectors, security guards, video cameras and other means of law enforcement in their schools, and my school had nothing. I approached my cooperating teacher about this and her answer surprised me greatly. She said the principal wanted the students to feel trusted coming to school, and wanted them to take ownership of their actions while spending time in school. Every day I had recess duty, there was a student wrestling a little too rough, or pushing too much, and even some verbal fights which turned into physical fights. However, I do not blame the kids for fighting when there is little to nothing available to play with on the school yard grounds during recess. These fights also happened inside school in the classroom, and could potentially be life threatening if they are not controlled quickly. I had to intervene in a student attacking another student with a pair of scissors, but because of my quick impulse, no one was hurt and the students were reprimanded.

The stereotypes of inner-city students are primarily accurate when we look at some of these students who are from single parent households, drug backgrounds, gang related influences, abuse, crime, and other circumstances that we only read about in the newspaper from time to time. Regardless of their background these students still have a large amount of potential in numerous aspects of their life. "The students in these inner-city settings were the most friendly and charismatic children I have ever worked with, and their needs are greater than most other children's needs; I was shown nothing but appreciation and gratitude for taking my time to be there."(Cromartie 2009) As teachers we cannot allow the stereotypes of these children and their living environment to affect our overall view or attitude towards them, we need to be accepting of their backgrounds and want them to strive to succeed and rise above the circumstances of their lives.

One of the questions which were addressed during our experience in Philadelphia was, "What was the most positive experience that you had working with urban students?" My most positive experience that I had working with urban kids was the passion and the drive that I brought out of them. Each time I walk into an urban setting I see a passion in the eyes of the children that I do not see in other classrooms. They appreciate my being there, and they need the attention and love more than other students. I feel that I have a special gift for working with inner-city children, and I loved to see the anxiousness and excitement in their eyes. One example in particular was a little boy I had. He roamed around the room and did not do his work until I got there. His desk was right beside mine and he loved me, he seemed to do anything I asked him. I would have him concentrate on his work, and he actually improved in the two weeks that I was there. It was very rewarding to know that I was able to make a difference in his life in just two weeks. This leads me to the above question, "If I can make a huge difference in the life of one child in two weeks, what can I do in the lives of twenty plus children in a school year?"(Garner, 2009)

The students that we were able to teach and work with during our experience in Philadelphia were ones that we as a group will hold near to our hearts for the rest of our lives. With only a little under two weeks in the field, we gained insight into the profession that not only is considered teaching, but rather touching children's lives forever. I do not feel as though I impacted the students as much as they impacted me. They impacted me with every glance, every word, and every action they took while I was in that classroom. "I feel as though working with those students not only did I help them, they helped me discover who I am and what I am meant to do with my life. Leaving those students broke my heart, and now I am even more convinced that this is what I want to do with my teaching career."(Garner, 2009) This experience gave many of us positive outlooks on teaching again, and inspired everyone of our group members. "Urban Seminar helped the three years in college I had prior to this experience make sense, it gave me a teacher's heart again, and made me care about my students in a deeper sense."(Brumfield, 2009)

We were not only in the classroom during our experience, but also were involved in many after school seminars, workshops, and even took a day off to tour Philadelphia. The speakers, including principals, former Urban Seminar students who are now teachers, authors, and other members of Philadelphia's school system all provided us with valuable insight and words of wisdom as many of us are graduating from college and looking towards our futures. "The lectures and workshops I attended offered incredible insight and advice into my field."(Cromartie, 2009) After long days at school seminars were not on the top of the list of things we wanted to do, but little did we know they were filled with valuable information that would change our opinions and views of inner-city students and the School District of Philadelphia in general. These provided us with question and answer sessions, freedom to express our feelings and emotions that we had going through the experience, and even allowed us to communicate with other students participating in the program. We established friendships among our peers that will last for a lifetime, and the bond we all share is our ability and willingness to teach in urban settings.

After coming home from this experience many of our Shippensburg University group members made the decision to follow their ambitions in becoming urban teachers. Most of us are still completing our college degrees, but none of us will forget our experiences in Philadelphia. While talking with my group members (Urban Seminar 2009) a common realization came about from all of us. That realization is the fact that Urban Seminar changed our lives forever, it not only provided us with the opportunity to branch out from our typical home lives, be exposed to situations that are predominantly in city schools, establish friendships with students from all over Pennsylvania, gain insight into our futures, but it primarily made us realize that this was the most authentic, rewarding experience of our educational lives thus far.

With every person I talked to from our group the response about Urban Seminar and the impact it made on our lives were very similar: "This was one of the greatest experiences that I've had at

Shippensburg University"(Muenker, 2009) "Participating in Urban Seminar was one of the best decisions I have ever made."(Leverentz, 2009) "This program makes anyone who takes part in it a better teacher and a better person."(Cromartie, 2009) I think that urban seminar is one of the best experiences that an education major could have."(Torre, 2009) "I must say that this experience was by far the best experience that any undergraduate student could ask for."(Brumfield, 2009) "Urban Seminar was without a doubt my best college experience yet."(Suchy, 2009) "This experience has definitely opened my eyes to all the complications and rewards of teaching. I feel as though I have started in a very challenging environment and that my experiences can only get better from here. Urban Seminar gave me a chance to experience firsthand life in the city, and the challenges of handling a classroom full of students with diverse backgrounds."(Garner, 2009)

Lastly I would like to share a story about one of the students in my classroom that has changed my life forever. William was a student that I honestly wrote off from my mind after the second day of school. He was a student who wandered around the room, refused to do his work, and really just distracted everyone around him all the time. I viewed him as a student who would not be able to be reached no matter how hard I tried. The looks he gave me were not welcoming at all, and looked more like I was going to be a burden in the classroom.

I watched him carefully throughout the first week and at the start of the second week. For some reason, each day I left the classroom William was on my mind, and I realized that I was not being fair by "writing him off." On Tuesday of the second week I decided to talk to William and attempt to help him concentrate in class. I started off the morning by saying good morning to him and asking him how his extended weekend was. He looked at me and replied, but did not go into much detail; it was as if he wanted to avoid confrontation. During Social Studies lesson that day I invited him back to my desk to help him with taking notes. I realized that when he began to write he could not spell, or even write for that matter. He was writing backwards, and could not seem to sound words out or even make meaning for words. It now made sense to me why he wanders around the room instead of writing or doing work. He had no problem answering questions aloud, but when it was time to write he stayed away from it.

William looked at me in a different way after I helped him that first day, and he even smiled at me at the end of the day. William was kicked out of his old school for fighting, and I can really tell that he has a side to him that if he is triggered, he goes wild. He has a look about him in his eyes that you can see the rage and anger form and then he reacts. Over the next couple of days he moved back and sat right beside me and really was focused on what he was doing. He did his work, and I even outlined notes for him to aid his learning. I feel as though a little extra help is all these students need to succeed.

Throughout the next several days I was there, I informed William that I was only going to be with him until Friday and then I had to leave, he had a really hard time with that. He looked at me like I was abandoning him and it broke my heart. I will think about William often, and really hope that he stays in school and will continue on the right path. It was amazing to me how much of a difference I made in one little boy's life in the two weeks that I was with him. Just the little bit of effort from a teacher proved to do wonders for this one child who needs attention. It is for this reason that I am striving to teach students in the urban setting. They are the ones who are in need of teachers who are not going to give up on them, and are going to give them those extra chances to succeed because they deserve it regardless of their past, or their lives outside school. These are the students who have the ability to make changes in not only their school, but in their community, their city, their state, their country, and potentially even the world if they choose to. Urban Seminar has given me the determination and the lifelong goal to reach these students in whatever way I can, and to make a difference in each of the children's lives I will encounter in my teaching career.

(Whitney Garner is a student at Shippensburg University.)

Chapter Two

Learning in Schools

In this chapter, participants in the Urban Seminar tell their stories of teaching and learning in the inner-city schools. Dawn Vose describes how her initial fears and misgivings gave way to a commitment and dedication to teaching. Kelly Espinosa reveals how student learning is connected with their social circumstances, and Jen McGinty illustrates what especial care and efforts may accomplish with these students. Reflecting on how she responded to a troubling question, Yolanda Hollock plodded us to think about how we would respond in similar situations. Jesse Wiser describes how he was able to make the leap from a textbook understanding of pedagogy to a real-world understanding of the power of connecting to his students' lives. Savanna Leninsky is impressed by her phenomenal teacher whose role model and classroom management strategies will stay with her wherever she teaches.

Not all of the stories are uplifting, however. Carrie Gutshall describes some of the challenges that teachers and children face every day in urban schools. Yet, despite those challenges, she reflects optimistically on the reality that all children, regardless of their circumstances, are capable of learning. Valerie Phipps reflects on the importance of mutual respect and understanding between teachers and students in establishing a supportive classroom environment. Finally, Eliza Altenderfer tells how her experience helped her overcome her initial tendency to feel sorry for her students and how she came to recognize that what her students needed was not her pity, but teachers who care and who are committed helping their students learn.

I am the One Who Needs Them
Dawn M. Vose

On May 17, 2009, my parents drove me through streets of Philadelphia to LaSalle University, where I would be staying for the next two weeks. I was filled with preconceptions and worries about where I would be living and in which school I would be placed. I was not sure what to expect of the coming weeks.

The previous January I realized I would not be graduating in five years as I had hoped. I switched my major, studied abroad, and had two majors in the past 4 years, and now I was 18 credits short to graduate from the five-year Dual Major Program in Early Childhood and Special Education. It so happened I heard about the Urban Seminar, offered to future teachers, which would replace the field portion of our High Block requirement. However, there was a waiting list at West Chester, and I was the eleventh person down the list; my chances of being chosen to participate were slim to none. It was not until the beginning of April when I got an e-mail from the Education Department asking if I was still interested in the program because those ahead of me had scheduled other classes and I was the next name on the list to attend the seminar. I was extremely excited, because this meant, as long as I could get into my second summer session class, I would be graduating the following May. I thought this seminar was just going to be an easy step to get me to graduation. Easy it was not!

When May 17th came I became as nervous as ever because I still had to earn these credits in an unfamiliar environment. Moving into the dorm room at LaSalle was overwhelming, but probably the simplest part of the next two weeks. We were to go to a meeting later that night, and jump right into teaching the next day with many meetings, journals, and lessons to write along the way. I was assigned to a school in the Central Region of Philadelphia, called DeBurgos Bilingual Elementary. The name alone added even more anxiety because I only knew a mere five words of Spanish, as I was informed that 90% of students in this school were from a Latino background.

The next morning, I went to the van that would take me to my placement. That morning, all of us who were assigned to DeBurgos sat in the van, fairly quiet as we drove through neglected houses, barred up windows, young children walking to school among the stunning murals that beautified the garbage filled and run down area where we would spend most of our next two weeks. It was very different than what I and the seven others in the van were used to seeing in our hometowns. I however, did not live far from Philadelphia, so I was a little more desensitized to our surroundings and not quite as shocked as my peers from other universities, but I was still nervous going into this situation. I had a fear of the unexpected and unknown and I did not know whether I would be able to connect with these children. One, because they were from a different cultural background and that they may have never had the childhood experiences I expect that most children get to, and two because I was not sure how to react to the lives and conditions these children live in each day. As a future teacher, my goal has always been to reach these children, to make a difference, and to let them know they have someone they could count on. I wanted to connect with these children. In a setting like this, I was doubting my abilities, I was doubting my will, and I was "feeling bad" for them.

Passing a beat up sign that said, Julia DeBurgos Bilingual Elementary, we saw a disheveled, vandalized building, missing windows, which looked more like a prison than a school for young children. Our hearts dropped and our fears were evident on all of our faces. However, our van driver, who was familiar with the area, kept driving. Two blocks away was the new, recently built, beautiful, bright, and welcoming elementary school with an open school yard, big open windows, and beautiful paintings. We all breathed a sigh of relief.

As we walked in through the school yard, all of the children stared at us, wondering who these strangers were and what it meant for them; just as we looked at them and wondered what they and the next two weeks would bring for us. We went into the office to meet our cooperating teachers, and wondered which grade we would teach and what kind of classroom it would be. I am a dual major in Early Childhood and Special Education, leaning more toward Special Education. So, I was hoping to be with children who had some special needs, which would cover the High Incidence Disability requirements in my program. However, when we went to pick up the children, I was very confused, because all of these children seemed as if they were all mainstreamed, regular education students, and they were third graders, which I have never had the experience of teaching before. I felt a moment of disappointment; I would later regret this feeling and become a different person because of these extraordinary children. The next two weeks were two of the most rewarding and influential times in my life.

As the kids entered Ms. Pond's classroom, they stood in a line and were each greeted, one by one, by Ms. Pond with a "High-five, hug, or handshake." I stood there, just smiling, because I knew that this little act, probably made these children feel so welcomed and started their day off so wonderfully. I knew that this was something I would do with my children some day, because I wanted them to feel so special and welcomed into "their" classroom every day. Then, as I was introduced to the children, I knew they could see the sense of nervousness on my face. But, they just smiled acceptingly at me and were so welcoming, that I felt a small sense of relief just looking out at all their little faces, which seemed to want this stranger's attention and were excited for what would be offered to them from her.

I soon began developing relationships with them as I walked around during lessons and offered help, listened to stories they told each other and shared with me, and questions they had throughout.

By the very next morning, they greeted me by name as I walked into the school yard. I felt so special. A few of them ran up and gave me a hug, and as Ms. Pond did her morning, "High-five, hug, or handshake," the quote on quote "bad kid" of the class turned around and gave me a hug, leading his other classmates to do the same. My heart filled with so much pride and awe. I thought to myself, "Are these the types of moments that make teachers' days and keep them going?" The "bad kid" soon became like my best friend. We had little inside jokes that was his way of letting me know that either something was bothering him or a way of keeping him out of trouble. Whenever he would want to do something mischievous, he would look back to see if I was looking first and if I was he would smirk and wait for a response from me. I would say things like, "Dude, what's up?" He would either talk to me or just giggle and go back to what was expected of him. Sometimes, he would come in from the school yard angry and unfocused; I thought he was just unmotivated and being a "typical" pre-teen. I did not know how to deal with a child when they act out like he had.

The next morning Ms. Pond let me in on his background, and the background of many of the students. Some of them had absent parents for no apparent reason at all, others had parents in and out of jail, some had parents who would take them out of school for no apparent reason at all other than they "felt like taking a three-week trip to Puerto Rico." There were so many stories that each of these children had going on in their personal lives. That morning, when they walked into the room, I held onto the hugs a few seconds longer; I looked at them with so much respect, and admittedly, a bit of guilt and sadness for them. I felt bad for them. I wanted to know these kids more, and wanted to fix all of their problems. I knew this was impossible, and soon realized that the best thing I could do for them, was to be the best possible teacher for those next two weeks, and to help them realize that school is a safe haven for them and that they had a few people who cared so much for them.

During these two weeks, I was supposed to learn about high incidence disabilities, but for me, my time there extended so far beyond just that. I connected with these children. I had the opportunity to work with one child who could barely speak English. She had a lot of difficulties with reading and comprehension. By the time I got done a one-on-one lesson with her, she was able to read the entire book front to back, and then summarize the entire story at the end and answer key questions throughout. I felt so proud, but not of myself, but for her. I said to her, "See, you can do it! How come you do not answer questions in class?" She answered, "Because I'm a dummy!" My heart broke and I assured her that no dummy could read a whole book, answer so many questions, and then summarize the whole book for me. One day she walked up to me, gave me the biggest hug, and looked up and said, "I love you; you are the best teacher ever! You are so nice!" I cannot put into words just how I felt at this moment!

Throughout my time there, I had the chance to sit and listen to teachers talk about the students at lunch, most of the time positively, but at times they needed to vent and seek advice from one another. They each depended on one another and worked so well on collaborating lesson plans, helping with extracurricular activities, and just offering their ear as a confidante. They were not just coworkers, but seemed like friends and a family-type community.

I had the chance to split up a fight between two boys; the bigger one crying at the end because he was not trying to be mean, but there was a deeper distress within him that I had yet to understand as to exactly where his anger was coming from. Later, I found out that he had a father in jail. I also sat in on a reinstatement of a child who was suspended for flipping desks and cursing out the teacher, however it was his solely Spanish speaking grandmother and baby sister that came to this meeting; his mother and father were not in the picture. One child was escorted to detention, picked up by, and disciplined by his sister, who was in eighth grade. These kids were some of the strongest people I have ever met. They had the strength to get up every day and come to school, with a smile on their faces. I could understand their behaviors now, but I also learned from Ms. Pond how to not let your feelings for what they are going through become an excuse to allow them to continue unacceptable behavior.

The day I left that school was so difficult. I went in on the morning of May 29th, anxious to be getting out of the dorm rooms, but so upset to be leaving this wonderful school, with such wonderful kids and faculty. I got up in front of the class that day and told them how wonderful I thought they all were, how thankful I was to have the opportunity to learn with them, and that if they set their minds to it they could do anything. I told them that I wanted to hear from Ms. Pond that they are all doing wonderfully in school, go on to high school, and one day make it on to college or a great career. I let them know that they truly changed me. All the kids ran up to take pictures with me, and as I looked over, "the bad kid," "the tough kid who got into a fight," and a few others had tears in their eyes, as did I, and then the "tough kid" burst into tears and gave me the biggest hug ever. I was so overjoyed and reassured. The children all asked if I could come back and visit or teach there like the student teacher they just had did. I told them how much I wish I could be with a group of kids like them. Saying goodbye, Ms. Pond told me that she would love if I applied to their school when I graduated, and that she thought I would be an asset to their special education program or even in their regular education program.

I walked out of that third grade classroom, down the hall to get my van, with my head held high but with tears in my eyes. A single tear rolled down my face as I looked back one last time and thought about how changed I felt because of this Seminar, because of this group of children and teachers. I sat the whole ride home wishing my time with them was longer. But, in just those two weeks, these kids changed my life. I was initially disappointed when I walked into my assignment, but once I met these kids and my cooperating teacher, I could not have asked for a better experience. This started off as a way to just get my credits and finish school, but by May 29, 2009, it was so much more! It sounds like a cliché, but this was a life changing experience for me and I could never thank them enough.

They helped me figure out the strength I had in me as a person and as a future teacher, and where exactly I belong as a teacher both location wise and in my philosophy, and my heart. I knew that I had truly found my calling. As a young, naïve woman, scared of her own shadow, worried and feeling sorry for these children living in this area, I no longer felt sorry for them, but envious of the strength, power and light I saw within them. I now knew that I belonged in the city of Philadelphia with *any* kind of children, special needs or not. I knew that I had the heart in me that these children needed; someone to care that extra little bit; someone they know they can count on. They needed me! But, more importantly, *I needed them!* For me, seeing the slightest progress made, or a little smile put on their face, THAT was the most rewarding feeling I have ever had in my life. They taught me so much about myself and helped me to figure out where exactly I was going in my career and in life. *They* are my inspiration. I thought these children needed someone to save them, I thought they needed me, but *I am the one who needed them.*

(Dawn M. Vose is a student at West Chester University.)

Two Hearts
Kelly Espinosa

– Kelly Espinosa,
Eugenio Maria de
Hostos Charter
School, Philadelphia

The most frequently asked question I get as a teacher in an urban setting is "What made you want to go there?" as if "there" is hell frozen over. As I get ready to tell them my answer, I see their sympathetic eyes gazing at me, feeling bad that I had no choice but to go "there." When I tell them that I chose to teach in a Title One school, their sympathetic voices often change to a monotone, one-word response of "oh," as if to say that I should not look to them for sympathy because it was my choice to work "there." What I normally do not tell people is that, if I am being honest with myself, I was exactly like them not too long ago. It was not until I was accidentally placed into the urban cohort at my university that I soon began to realize just how special it is to teach children in urban settings. Although I have had many impressionable students who have made me realize what a privilege it is to teach them every day, my most impressionable student to this date was a child whom I met during the Philadelphia Urban Seminar, which I attended during my junior year of college. This is the reason why I decided to begin a wonderful, rewarding career in a very special place.

Walking into my Northeast Philadelphia school for the Urban Seminar was quite an eye opener. Despite the fact that I live only an hour outside of the city, I had never been truly immersed in North Philadelphia. There were no grassy spots, no playgrounds, and lots of trash. I was bracing myself for what I was about to find inside, however, I quickly felt my cheeks redden as I realized it looked "normal" on the inside. I was greeted by a wonderful teacher with whom I was to work for two weeks in her bilingual kindergarten class. I nervously stood, tapping my feet, bracing myself for twenty-some Spanish-speaking five and six year olds to enter the classroom. I was instantly drawn to their warm smiles and their true academic talent. While working with the students throughout the day, I could not help but notice one little boy in particular, one to whom I was drawn for his big smile and his obsession with drawing hearts.

I used to sit by this little boy and watch him draw hearts of all different shapes, sizes and colors. I envisioned him imagining his favorite play spot, his warm bed, and ice cream cones. I could not have been more wrong.

It was while working with this little boy that I learned my first lesson in being naïve. I am a huge believer in the fact that children give us messages every day, not only through their words, but through their actions as well. As it turns out, I was not paying close enough attention to this particular child's message. This little boy was drawing hearts in memory of his mother, who he thought was dead.

Being one of at least six children, this little boy had a whole lot of love and attention given to him at every minute of the day. However, shortly before the winter holidays, the little boy's life took a dramatic turn when his father became ill. Wanting to rest in peace in his native country, his father returned to Puerto Rico. But the family was only able to afford one plane ticket, so the mother had to stay behind. Distraught at the loss of her husband and not knowing how to properly grieve, the mother of this little boy became involved with a new group of friends and started a reckless life. Late on, when their housing payments were due, the landlord of the building in which the family resided went to check up on them. He did not find the mother, instead, he found six children left alone.

Confronted with a legal and moral responsibility, the landlord called the police who showed up at the door with a Social Service person. As the Social Services person was rounding up the children, the mother returned home. Enraged, she ran up the stairs and returned with a large knife, swinging it at police officers and threatening to kill someone if her children were to be taken away. At this point, the police shot the little boy's mother, and the whole scene played out in front of the children's frightened eyes.

Soon after the tragedy, the children were separated in pairs and placed into foster homes. Not being able to have contact with their mother, the children assumed their mother was dead.

I will never forget being told this story for the first time, eating my granola bar and sitting on the small kindergarten chair. I do not remember crying. At that point the shock had not subsided. I thought that these were things you heard about in the movies. Or, worse yet, the things you do not take the time to listen to because your own ignorance tells you it would never happen where you live.

As I looked on at the faces of the wide-eyed, tiny kindergartners on the last day of my two-week experience, I felt emptiness in my heart. It was an emptiness that I could not help but feel because of the twenty-some kindergartners to whom I had become attached and would most likely not see again. As the students each handed me cards thanking me for my time spent with them, I could not help but immediately look at the letter of the little boy to whom I had become so drawn. At the bottom of the letter, there was a new picture. Not the familiar hearts that I was used to seeing, but a little boy and a little girl holding hands. When I asked him whom the picture depicted, he answered with a smile on his face, "Yo y usted," or "Me and you" in English. The tears began to run down my face as I realized it was the first picture he drew of something other than hearts since his mother was shot.

There is not a day that goes by that I do not think about the boy who deeply touched my heart. This is why I am a teacher in an urban setting. It is these innocent faces who will give you more love than you ever thought possible. It is due to this heart-drawing boy and other children like him that I was able to drop my stereotyping of the city and the children who are raised in it. There are thousands of other students just like this little boy in our school systems that need our love and respect. These students are resilient, intelligent, and have more love to give than most. Realizing the effect I had on one student in such a short time tells me that there are many other students just like him who have experienced more in their short lives than I have in my 23 years. These students need to feel loved and cared for and I have a whole lot of love to give.

(Kelly Espinosa is teacher at Eugenio Maria de Hostos Charter School in Philadelphia.)

"Hi Miss Jen"
Jen McGinty

When I signed up to be part of the Urban Seminar, I did not know what to expect. I have worked with many children with different types of disabilities, but never in an inner-city setting. I grew up in Northeast Philadelphia and moved in 7th grade, but I knew this experience would be a little different from the one I had. I was assigned to a 7th and 8th grade Learning Support classroom in the Northwest region of Philadelphia and was a little intimidated at first. Why was I intimidated?

I walked into the classroom and did not feel immediately accepted by any of the children in the classroom. I was shorter than just about every student in the classroom. In addition, besides the teacher, I was the only white person in the classroom. Within seconds I realized that these two weeks were going to be a unique experience I would never forget. Whether it would turn out to be a good or bad one was yet to be seen!

The entire first week was the Carnival Week which involved music, dancing, games, and lots of food on the playground outside the school. I was amazed at how open and fun this atmosphere seemed to be for the students. There was music playing and the kids were dancing and playing games. I had to stop the urge to go crazy and dance because I needed to be professional! I did rock a few moves from behind my Snow Cone station and occasionally saw another teacher doing the same at her Cotton Candy station. It was a blast!

I have never been in a school where there was so much organized chaos and noise. However, I have also never been in a school where the students were having so much fun! This entire week was a treat for the students to reward them for their efforts throughout the school year.

The younger students came outside in the morning and the older students came out in the afternoon. The younger students were paired up with an older student who would watch them and help them give their tickets in exchange for food, drinks, and games. My job was to make the snow cones for the hundreds of students who would come through my line that day. I was definitely not dressed appropriately so the principal was nice enough to give me a spare shirt of hers that she had lying around in a drawer in her office. In no other field experience has a principal taken the time to converse with me, let alone give me a shirt of hers to keep. Talk about acceptance and feeling like a part of the staff right away!

Making snow cones proved to be an awesome experience and I discovered I am a pretty talented ice scooper. The best part about giving out snow cones was being able to greet almost every student in the school. It is tough to imagine, but by the end of my two weeks at Henry, I recognized just about every student in the school. It was an unbelievable feeling to be walking down the hallway and hear students I might have only met once, scream "Ms. McGinty" or "Miss Jen!"

Inside the school, the students were creating posters, preparing food and presentations to represent the country which their classes chose to learn more about for International Day. The students traveled to each class and listened to the presentations, then ate the food that had been prepared by that class and which was native to their assigned country. My class had chosen India and, until this event, their only experience with the country had been enjoying Indian food. That was the day that I tried curry for the first time in my life. When it was finally time to buckle down and get to work after a fun filled week, I really got to see what teaching in the urban setting was about. In my 7th and 8th grade learning support class, there were nine students, all of whom were African American, except for one boy, who was Latino. The students were reading the book, "The Giver" and did not seem to enjoy it very much. They would take turns reading out loud, and although they could get through the reading, they did not understand the text. Two boys in the class would fall asleep everyday during the reading of this book. I sympathized with them because I knew this book was above their reading and comprehension level, and to make it even worse, they could not relate to the text. When I sat next to one of the boys to help him read, he complained and said "I can't stay awake! It's like a bedtime story book!"

Helping the student who complained about the book understand and comprehend it proved to be a rewarding experience in itself. While he was reading I was sitting next to him and listening.

I would stop him after a few paragraphs and talk to him about what he read. Most of the time he had little to no idea about what he read so I would help him comprehend the text by going back and rereading a few sentences for him and talking him through its meaning.

After we finished reading, the teacher began asking the class questions about what they had just read. This boy, who would have normally been sleeping or not participating during these conversations, was raising his hand high in the air, waving it from side to side, begging the teacher to call on him for the answer. I sat back and watched this child enjoy reading this book for the very first time. How I felt at that moment is something I will never forget. In the short period of time that I had to work with this child, it made that much of a difference.

Math is my strongest subject so I was excited to help these students with the math work they were given to complete. Although all of the students were given the same work, many of them were on very different skill levels. I was able to circulate around the room and help almost every student with math problems with which they were struggling. The strategy that seemed to work best with these students was repetition through the spiral method. The more problems I helped them with individually, the better they completed the problems independently. I was happy to have been so helpful to them, but saddened by the thought that they do not have enough support in the class to assist them in the way the teacher and I could when there were two of us in the classroom.

When the special education teacher in the 5th and 6th grade learning support class next door was absent, the substitute teacher asked me to assist her in the classroom after seeing the way I interacted with those students. Of course I was flattered and wanted to help in any way that I could, but I was enjoying getting to know my 7th and 8th grade students and was not too excited about cutting that time short when I only had a few days left with them. Although I was upset leaving my students, I assumed there would be a lot of knowledge and experience to gain from being in a different classroom as well. I had no idea how right my assumption was.

Walking into this chaotic classroom made me realize how well behaved my 7th and 8th grade students really were. Suddenly the occasional hitting, name-calling, and throwing of different objects I experienced in my 7th and 8th grade class seemed to be relatively controlled behavior compared to what was occurring in this class. The students were extremely disrespectful to the substitute and even more so to each other. I had to break up three arguments which could have escalated to the students' fighting. I noticed that these students, even though they would never admit it, needed structure and missed their teacher. To make the situation even worse, their teacher had left no plans for the substitute so she had no clue about what to do with them.

One particular student, who is normally tough for his own teacher, was playing games with the substitute that just about pushed her over the edge. Lesson number one learned from this experience: yelling at the students and threatening them with no intention to follow through with those threats never works. The substitute got so fed up with this one student that she made me bring him down to the principal. I did not agree with this because I felt like there could have been other steps taken before it needed to escalate to sending him to the office.

The principal brought him back up to the class about 30 minutes later and warned him and the rest of the class that she would call their parents if she heard any more about their misbehavior. Within five minutes of the student's returning she caught him with sunflower seeds in his pocket and ordered him to go back down to the principal's office. This was absolutely ridiculous. That student and I both understood that being sent to the principal again would be the next consequence if he were to act up again. But he had not acted up. It was quite obvious that the substitute teacher was annoyed with him because of his earlier misbehavior and just wanted him out of the class for good. I got up with the student and walked him out of the classroom, trying to discuss the situation with him in the hallway. He started to cry and could not understand what he had done wrong and seemed scared at the thought of his parents being called. I picked up on these emotions and realized that maybe there could be another consequence for this student, one which would be more appropriate given the nature of the behavior that resulted in him being sent out of the classroom.

The students in the learning support class I was normally in next door were at lunch, so that teacher stepped in with a consequence that she and I felt was more appropriate. The boy was raging with emotions and she knew he could not go back into that classroom. After discussing with her how his day had been going and explaining to her the reasons why he was kicked out of the class, she decided he would be best accommodated in her classroom while the other students were gone. She negotiated with him and told him that she would allow him to sit in her classroom to blow off some steam, but when he entered his classroom again he needed to apologize to the substitute teacher and stay well behaved the rest of the day. If he were to break that promise, there was no other option for him than to be sent to the principal's office, which would result in the calling of his mother. Within 40 minutes, he had calmed down, apologized to the teacher, and resumed his day back in his classroom. He did not have another occurrence of bad behavior after that.

When this situation was over, my cooperating teacher thought it would be best for me to come back into her classroom. She told me that it was not my responsibility to be dealing with the behaviors in that classroom because that is why the substitute was there and also that my 7th and 8th grade students were asking about me and missed me. I was ecstatic to hear this. After just experiencing why some teachers experience "burn-out" so quickly in inner-city schools, I now saw these students in a different light and constantly praised their efforts and work ethic.

All of the participants in the Urban Seminar received tee shirts that said *We Are the Urban Seminar* on the front. I had all of the students in my class sign my shirt so that I could take a memory of each student with me. I thought that they would just sign their names and pass the shirt to the next person. To my surprise, each student also wrote a personal message. I observed them as they sat and thought for a moment before writing as if they were really trying to think of the perfect message to write. One of the most common messages written on my shirt was "Please come back."

I have to tell you, these messages touched me so deeply. I go to school in West Chester, Pennsylvania, and most of the experiences I accumulated have been in predominantly white suburban schools. Every experience I have had was amazing and I carry with me many memories from those experiences. The difference of those previous experiences, compared to this one, was that in those schools, the children knew I was there and if I was not, someone else would be. These Philadelphia students truly appreciated me being there and knew that someone like me might probably not come along that often. And if they did, they would leave and never come back as I am sure many teachers have in the past.

The night before my last day of the field experience I stayed up until 3:00 am making a thank you poster for my students and mentally preparing me for, what I presumed would be, an emotional goodbye. My poster had a huge thank you note at the top with their pictures and names all over. At the bottom I wrote a more personal message to the students encouraging them all to never give up and to always try their hardest! They all loved it! Along with the poster I brought in each student's favorite doughnut and a pack of 100 mechanical pencils. The students only had enough room on their tiny yellow #2 pencils to fit about two, maybe three, of their finger tips around it for grip.

My biggest realization came when I distributed these mechanical pencils. To tell you the truth, I was nervous about distributing pencils because I thought the class would think it was a lame gift. However, every student in the class was excited to be able to choose their own colors and to have their very own mechanical pencils. It was obvious some of these students had never used a mechanical pencil as they made the common mistake of exposing too much graphite where their pencil point would immediately break. I walked around and observed two students struggling to figure out how to get the graphite to come out again. I watched them as they twisted and turned the ends of the pencils in frustration. Something so small I take for granted every day, these students never had the chance to experience, until now. I gave them that experience and I could tell they truly appreciated it.

What did I take from seeing their messages asking me to please come back? I gave my word that I would be back, and soon they would see how special they were to me. I gave my students my email address before leaving, in the hope that they would email me and I could be some sort of an outlet for them. I was hoping that I could be a person they would feel safe turning to talk to if they felt they had no one else. Within about a week of my leaving, I received an email from one of my students. It just read "Hi Miss Jen." For some strange reason, just that small email made me light up inside. Out of all of the times I have given my field students my email address, this is the first time a student has emailed me back.

A few days after receiving that email, and many more from that student, another student emailed me and told me he missed me. I knew then, no matter how small, I made a difference in the little time I spent with them.

I told a few of my students and my cooperating teacher that I would be attending their school's graduation on June 19, 2009. As the days approached I became more and more excited to see my students graduate and move on to the high schools of their choice. For as much happiness I felt for them, I was worried too. I knew that my students, all of whom have learning disabilities, were going to enter general education classes where they will be pretty far behind their peers. My biggest fear for them was that they might be discriminated against by their peers, and that they would become discouraged and make the decision to quit school.

On the morning of the graduation, I left my house at 8:00 am because I wanted to make sure there would be no traffic that could make me late for this ceremony which was scheduled to begin at

9:30 am. I pulled up to the Germantown Jewish Centre, where the graduation was being held, at 8:45 am. The graduation was being held in this building that was five minutes from the school because the school did not have a big enough auditorium to accommodate the event.

I walked into the building and was immediately greeted by the teachers from my school who were anxiously awaiting the students' and parents' arrival. Most of the teachers looked at me with disbelief that I had come for the graduation. One of the teachers looked at me and said, "You are so supportive." I just told her, "I could not miss it."

I took my seat and waited for the students to arrive. It was not long before I heard, "Alyshia, look. Miss Jen is here!" Two of the girls from my class came over and gave me a hug. They looked so beautiful in their dresses, and I let them know it right away. They thanked me for coming and gave me the biggest smiles then reported to the line in which they would soon be walking. Eventually, everyone took their seats and the ceremony began.

All of the graduating students walked down the middle aisle to the front of the auditorium and stood in front of the large crowd which consisted of parents, teachers, and peers. All of them stood tall with such pride and confidence. The teachers took turns coming to the front of the crowd and announcing awards that some of the students were chosen to receive. The early awards were the most common awards where nearly every student received something. The most prestigious awards were given at the end.

Many of the students from my class received awards for their outstanding effort in specific academic areas and specials they were involved in at school. My eyes were already full of tears, but I refused to let them fall. I do not really know why I was afraid to let them fall. I think I was worried that the parents present who did not know me might wonder why I was crying before they were.

The teachers came up and shared their prepared speeches before each of the big awards was given. One of the teachers cried as she struggled to give her speech for the student chosen for one of the school's most prestigious awards that is given in honor of a fellow student who was now deceased. The most prestigious award is given to one student each year that persevered and made the greatest effort from the graduating class. The teacher was crying as she described the student receiving the award as someone who she "will miss dearly and who has been and always will be so special to her." Trying to pull myself together after such a beautiful speech, I lost it when she called the name of a student in my class. The same boy who just a few days earlier I was helping to read "The Giver" was now receiving the most prestigious award the school has to offer. All 4 foot 10 inches, in a charming all white tuxedo, he proudly marched to the front of that auditorium with his head held so high, and grasped tightly the award he most definitely had earned.

I can best describe my emotions at this time to have gone from just tears of joy to utter bliss. My heart hurt and my hands had needle-like pains shooting through them because of the overwhelming emotions, which at this moment, ran throughout my entire body. I was so proud of him. It was emotional just thinking about the obstacles this child has had to overcome because of his disability and that he was now receiving an award, not only for overcoming those obstacles, but also for making an impact on others as he did so. This experience finally opened my eyes to what teaching in the inner-city is all about.

These two weeks taught me so much about myself and the type of person and teacher I want to become. The inner-city schooling environment is so raw and the experiences a teacher can gain from this are infinite. From this experience, I learned that each day of teaching in an inner-city school is a challenge in itself, but is also immensely rewarding. This is the place where great teachers are needed and will make the most difference. These are the children that are sometimes left behind. These are the children, who if given a chance, can and will succeed to unbelievable heights.

(Jen McGinty is a student at West Chester University.)

Social Studies as Conscientization: Discussing Puerto Rican History with Puerto Rican Teenagers
Jesse Wiser

When you know your history
Then you will know where you're coming from
Then you won't have to ask me
Who the 'ell do you think I am?

Bob Marley's "Buffalo Soldier"

Who did I think I was—a white, lifetime small-town-resident, college student standing in front of twenty-five Latino eighth graders in the heart of Philadelphia, leading a class discussion on the history of a people I had never studied, whose grandchildren were sitting attentively before me, eyes glued on me as though I was the world's foremost Hispanic historian? Who was I to describe, in details gleaned from an online research paper, how people like them had struggled against oppression by people like me?

These questions had gnawed on my mind as I scoured the Internet for information on Sonia Sotomayor and highlighted copies of Pedro Pietri's "Puerto Rican Obituary" in preparation for this lesson. Yet they disappeared the instant I introduced the lesson to the class. The young men and women, who had every right and reason to treat me as an impostor, who themselves live the lives of the people that I, a complete outsider, had chosen to discuss, were riveted. Not because I displayed knowledge or eloquence, but because I provided an opportunity for them to discover meaning by studying history.

Faced with the daunting assignment of teaching at least one ninety-minute lesson to Mrs. Cohen's eighth grade social studies class, I submitted several possibilities to my mentor teacher that reflected my major areas of historical study and somewhat related to the chapter of United States history that the class was currently studying. It was to be my first lesson in front of a completely non-white class in an urban school, and I was playing it safe. Mrs. Cohen offered a few words of critical praise for my lesson planning efforts. Then she threw me a curve ball: "I'm not sure how much they know about their *own* history." Meaning: That is your lesson!

I was quite sure that I knew next to nothing about the history of Puerto Rican immigrants, whose grandchildren and great-grandchildren comprised over ninety percent of Mrs. Cohen's students. I knew of, but little about, the militant Young Lords Party; I admired the slugger Roberto Clemente, who died transporting aid to Central America; and I discovered the existence of the poet Julia DeBurgos when I received my placement at this Philadelphia school which bears her name. How could I walk into this academic consulate of Puerto Rico the next morning with a ninety-minute lesson on Puerto Rican history? I was an outsider in every way. How could I presume to "teach" these bright youngsters about the lives of urban Puerto Ricans when, by virtue of their daily existence, they knew far more than I could learn in a lifetime, let alone one evening?

Before I even thought to protest however, Paulo Freire's conscientization approach surged through my mind. Here was an opportunity to have a conversation with the students that they might find meaningful. Rather than fret over the differences in our perspectives, I could offer my thoughts, draw out theirs, and steer them to search for meaning about their people from the past. If I showed my students that I was interested in them, their history, and their thoughts and ideas pertaining to their heritage, perhaps they would view me less as a pretentious outsider. Might they gain an insight from studying their people's history in ways that they could apply to their own lives? With these thoughts in mind, I set to work collecting material and arrived the next morning with a satisfactory lesson.

I began by asking the students whether any of them knew when and why their grandparents or other relatives had come to Philadelphia. To my surprise, not a single hand went up. As I was to discover more and more as the lesson progressed, very few of these young people had ever been exposed to even the slightest elements of their ethnicity's history or culture. I began to realize that I *was* introducing them to new information, which they eagerly soaked up. As I posed questions to stimulate discussion, I found the students to be remarkably perceptive in understanding and evaluating the lives and actions of their Puerto Rican predecessors. They were doing exactly what I had hoped they would—analyzing the past to discover meaning.

Five volunteer students stood in front of the class, reading the poem "Puerto Rican Obituary" by Pedro Pietri, a Puerto Rican poet of whom none of them had ever heard. Scanning copies of the poem, which I had divided into parts and highlighted, these five recreated the anxieties and frustrations of the Puerto Rican immigrant community of Spanish Harlem:

Juan: Here lies Juan
Marcos: Here lies Miguel
Grisella: Here lies Milagros
Crystal: Here lies Olga
Lynette: Here lies Manuel
All: who died yesterday today
and will die again tomorrow
Juan: Always broke
Marcos: Always owing
Grisella: Never knowing
that they are beautiful people
Lynette: Never knowing
the geography of their complexion
All: PUERTO RICO IS A BEAUTIFUL PLACE!
PUERTORRIQUENOS ARE A BEAUTIFUL RACE!

As we discussed Pietri's work, one concept seemed difficult for the students to digest: Juan, Miguel, Milagros, Olga and Manuel, and the thousands of immigrants they represent in the poem, tried to escape their ethnicity, culture, language, and place of origin to avoid the social stigma preventing their success. My students insisted that one's heritage should be a source of pride: "If you know who you are, then nobody is going to tell you something else." I could only agree.

However, only a handful were able to list the three roots of their Puerto Rican ethnicity—Taino, Spanish, and African—and this presented me with an opportunity to connect the students with something positive happening in their own neighborhood. The previous week, I had visited a community-based cultural center only a dozen blocks from the school, where several elderly women have constructed gardens representing each of these ethnic roots in an effort to keep Puerto Rican heritage alive, as well as maintaining an eco-friendly island of organic food production. When I described this cultural center to my students, I found that only one girl even knew of its existence. However, many others expressed interest and enthusiastically promised to check it out and get involved. Who can tell whether our class discussion on the value of one's heritage would not spark an enduring desire in even one student to work for cultural promotion in the future?

The lesson that I had planned for one period stretched into a second, in which we analyzed the actions and goals of the Young Lords Party, and a third, in which we examined Sonia Sotomayor's attributes as a potential Supreme Court Justice. During the course of the lesson, my anxieties over whether the students would accept me, an ethnic outsider, as a teacher of their history evaporated. My confidence as a teacher grew with the students' confidence as "organic intellectuals," in Freirean terminology, who could apply their own perspectives to the subject matter. In fact, our positions as teacher and students shifted, for I was not merely depositing information. Rather, we were sharing together the experience of exploring meaning in history.

I will never know whether my three days of discussing Puerto Rican history with Puerto Rican teenagers will have any sort of impact on their lives. For many of them, academics are a secondary concern to the difficulties of daily life in the inner city, and my lessons might be quickly forgotten along with the rest of United States history. However, I do believe that discovering, studying and understanding one's history can be a form of conscientization, in which one applies a critical, questioning search for solutions to life's hardships and frustrations. My students showed me that they can apply this approach in the classroom. May the meaning that they found through our discussions of the past empower them to make critical and conscious decisions about their future.

(Jesse Wiser is a student at California University of PA.)

"I'll always be small."
Yolanda Hollock

My first time being in a third-grade urban elementary classroom was probably one of the most meaningful experiences I have had so far in my life. I went into the classroom with the prior knowledge that these students are bad, they live in the "ghetto," that they do not make it past a certain grade because they get caught up with what is going on in the streets, that they have parents who do not care, and that they live their lives as a constant battle. Having the opportunity to be involved for even just a short period of time in an urban school district, does have its ups and downs. The students are always coming to school every day, so that is an up. But when a ten-year-old boy tells me he will never be big because he is going to be shot and killed, that is one of the downs of being a teacher in an urban school.

I was walking in the hallway with my class while talking and joking with some of them. I did it intentionally because I wanted the students to be able to laugh about things and did not always have to be serious. One boy had on his big grey puffy jacket because it was cold when we went out for recess. I told him he could be called "big grey." He replied with "Miss, that's my favorite color." At this point I was thinking to myself "hey, he is opening up to me, so I had better keep talking." I replied with "Well, since I have grey on and it is your favorite color, I will be big grey and you could be little grey." He looked at me and said, "I'll always be small." I asked, "Why? You will be big in a few years." He said, "No, I'll always be small; I'll never be big because I'll get shot and killed on the streets."

Now, since you just read this, are you thinking of all the ways you would tell a child why he should not be thinking this way? If your answer is yes, good! Because I feel that in an urban school district you would need to have quick reactions to such comments. So, for me, hearing this for the first time ever, I wondered what I could possibly say to alter this child's state of mind. Who am I? Some "white girl from the suburbs" who is walking into a situation about which she knows very little. Do I lie and tell him everything will be "OK," or do I disrespect his community and say it is better outside of the inner-city? How do I, "the white girl from the suburbs," really know what this child's fate will be in the future? I only know what I learned where I grew up, which was the suburbs, and he knows what he learned on the streets of his neighborhood.

You are probably wondering what my response was? My response was, "Stay away from people and situations that may cause that to happen to you." He said, "Maybe."

Now, was my response similar to, or different from what yours would have been? How could I have approached it differently? Should I have said something else, maybe something more persuasive or meaningful? After I gave my response I had time to reflect on it in the classroom, badgering myself. Was it a good answer, did it show I cared? I really just wanted that student to know that I cared! Since then, as I have told this story to my friends who are also in the education program, I was looking for answers to my question. What I usually got back was the "Oh My God!" look. I feel that I received that look because, like me, they wondered how you could possibly respond to something like that. It also frustrates me because I want their opinions; I want to know what they think. But I did not receive any feedback. For days, I would just think about it to the point where I would just shake my head in dismay because a ten-year-old boy should not be living in such fear. I remember when I was ten years old, that thought would never have crossed my mind. I was just worrying about fitting in and about the fear of rejection from my classmates. I thought those were the worst things that could happen, but obviously there are worse things.

The class had a "special" late that day. The teacher was very nice and at the end of the class I ended up telling him about my experience so far. I did bring up what the boy said and the teacher's reply was, "It's the norm." I received a reply of "It's the norm." I have heard that excuse so many times here, I feel like my head is spinning. Instead of just saying "Oh, it's the norm," why does no one choose to fix it, or do something about it? It does not have to be the norm. People need to initiate and lead changes.

President Obama wants change, so why can the children who are living in constant fear of the street not have their change? I understand that it is hard to change a city and I do not expect it to be done overnight. But with patience and caring, something can be done about the situation in which these children live. The teacher was also telling me that when the children walk the streets; they know how to scan the streets to see if they are safe. The children also know how to look over their shoulders, and know when to dodge from danger when it is in front of them.

Now, you may be asking "Why?" or just shaking your head that this cannot be true. How can a city that cares so much for their children let things get this bad? Is it that response "It is the norm" that allows this to occur? This situation did not happen overnight. It happened gradually and no one stopped it. I understand that people can make a difference in their community, but there still exists the constant battle of fear that is in that child's mind walking home from school or walking anywhere in their neighborhood. I hope that one day; someone will make a change and walk past those barriers to make a difference for these children. These children, like all children, need to walk without fear; they need to walk knowing that they will be safe. Why should a ten-year-old boy, or at any age for that matter, need to know how to scan a street for danger and be able to dodge trouble? Why? Why should an urban child feel this way? Why can they not just go to school to learn and not fear walking down a street? These are the many questions that I have been asking myself lately…why? A ten-year-old boy, with such potential to be anything he wants to be in life, should not fear death. He should not have to live in fear. These are our children and childhood should be their time to be free, have fun, and not live in fear.

I admit that, over the years, I was not the best student in school, but I was tired of teachers making judgments about me saying that I would not go anywhere in life and that I was lazy. I felt that I was having a constant battle with myself to prove them wrong all the time. If I fail at something, I beat myself up about it. But, when I achieve something, I want them to know they were wrong about me. I do not and will not ever judge my students, because that is not what a teacher should be, especially in an urban school district. Students want someone who cares, shows them respect, and gives them knowledge to better themselves for the future. I know that I can do it and that I will do it. Many of these students have already been judged on the basis of their race and situation and have already been labeled as "going nowhere fast." So here I am, 23 years old, a White/Italian future urban school district teacher, trying to preach change. Will I succeed? Yes! Why? Because these children deserve the best, and nothing but the best, and will be taught to the best of what I am capable of offering. I want my future students to achieve, and do well. If I saved myself from the wrong path and went into a profession that almost failed me as a child, there will be change. I will save my future students. Why? It is my norm!

(Yolanda Hollock is a student at Bloomsburg University.)

Philadelphia Urban Experience: A Phenomenal Teacher
Savanna Leninsky

What do you picture when you think of an inner-city school? Do you see disrespectful students arguing and fighting, a teacher with no control of her classroom, dull classrooms with limited materials and deteriorating facilities? Before my trip to Philadelphia, that was what I had envisioned; however the reality was far from that image. I attended an elementary school in Central East Philadelphia, and was placed in a kindergarten classroom. There were twenty Hispanic and African-American students, and my mentor teacher had been teaching for twenty-four years.

Throughout the two weeks, I had a great experience observing and working with a wonderful, hardworking, and caring teacher. I observed my mentor teacher's classroom management, teaching skills, and planning techniques. I also observed her relationships with students, colleagues, parents, and volunteers. She gave me guidance on room setup and answered my questions with wisdom from her years of experience. These two weeks provided me with insight on teaching and most importantly a new perspective on urban school districts and communities.

Classroom Setup

When arriving at the school for the first time, I saw the opposite of what I had expected. While walking to my classroom, I noticed that although the building was old, it seemed comfortable and filled with school spirit. The classroom was full of color and pictures, with ornaments hanging from the ceiling, and books all around. There were four large color-coded desks that corresponded with a supply shelf behind the desks. The colors were basic: red, blue, green, and yellow. There were also cubbies for each student's work and shelves for their jackets and book bags.

The classroom had a large carpeted area (where most of the class time was spent), with interesting lines of different colors and squares. Each student was assigned a colored square in which they sit. I liked that the students could sit in "their seat" and still be interactive. I also liked the game spots my mentor teacher placed on the carpet. This is where the students would create a square to participate in math, literacy game, and other activities.

Lastly, there were thirteen different educational workstations (centers) that were color-coded around the classroom. I was amazed by the organization. These stations were used daily with two or three different rotations for about twenty-minute rounds. I enjoyed working with the kindergarteners during this time. It was a nice way to get to know the children and work with their different educational levels. The workstations included spelling, the alphabet, reading (100-Book Challenge), writing and doodling, listening and math. Each workstation had an educational purpose, most of which focused on literacy.

Classroom Management

Most of my learning during the two weeks involved classroom management. The teacher had complete control of her classroom through intrinsic and extrinsic motivational strategies. She also used class rules and other management skills to facilitate student learning.

Classroom Rules. The teacher's classroom rules were clear and understood by the students. She made sure the students followed the rules and they knew there would be consequences if they did not. The rules were hung in the front of the classroom and they included: 1. Move carefully, 2. Work carefully and clean up, 3. Be kind all the time, 4. Be an excellent reader and 5. Stay on the job.

Job Chart. To keep the classroom organized and give the students responsibility, the teacher had a job chart. It included different jobs to which the students were assigned weekly. If the students did not follow the job responsibilities correctly, they were "fired." The jobs included line leader (one boy and one girl), messengers, coat/book bag hangers, chair helpers, and cubby checkers. These jobs were simple, yet they required the students to take responsibility and use organizational techniques in the classroom.

Good Notes. At the end of each day, the students received a good note if they followed the rules throughout the day. The good note was stamped with the date. To help with classroom management and for the students to earn a good note there was a chart hanging in the classroom. The chart had a beginning level and three levels below. The chart was called "I am following our rules today" and the levels included: 1. I needed a reminder to stay on the job, 2. I needed more help to follow our rules, and 3. No good note today; I will try harder tomorrow.

At the beginning level each student had a clothespin with his or her number on it. If they did not stay on task or listen their pin would be moved down a level. If the pin reached the third level a good note would not be sent home for the day. If all of the students' clothespins stayed at the beginning level the teacher would bake cupcakes for the next day.

During my two-week visit to this classroom, I was lucky to see the students accomplish this goal. On the day of the kindergarten field trip to see *Rapunzel,* all of the students were on their best behavior and followed the rules. I saw the children work together to earn the cupcakes.

At the end of each day, the students count their good notes. Each student brings his/her bag to the front of the classroom, and as a class, they count the good notes. If the student has received ten good notes, they can choose a prize from the treasure box.

Boot Camp. Throughout the day most of the work was done on the carpet completing hands-on activities or working at stations. Even when the students worked in their journals, they sat throughout the classroom and were free to walk around to use their vocabulary books and words around the room for spelling. Both the teacher and students enjoyed working hands-on more than working quietly at their desks. If the classroom became out of hand, my mentor teacher would hold a "boot camp." This consisted of the students sitting at their desks working on papers quietly.

During my two weeks in the classroom, I saw the students participate in a boot camp. The day before they participated in it the students were very talkative and uncooperative. To help the students understand that they need to cooperate, the teacher held a boot camp the following morning. During the boot camp the students respected the teacher's request and understood why they were participating in this boot camp. I could tell the students did not enjoy this time but they did learn from it.

Motivation. Throughout the class, the teacher used many extrinsic motivations such as the good notes, treasure box, cupcakes, and boot camp and so on. What I especially liked about this teacher's motivation strategies was the amount of intrinsic motivation tactics she also used. Over the two weeks I noticed the teacher using techniques such as shaking hands with the students and giving encouragement. I could tell this worked just as well because of the students' reactions and smiles. During lessons I would notice the teacher giving different types of "good jobs." She found a different way to show excitement and how proud she was of each student. I was amazed by the variety of management and motivation techniques she had used.

Student Reaction. Over the two weeks, I could see how my mentor teacher's classroom management affected the students. I could see how hard the students worked and respected her. They also respected each other, which made the class more like a family. I noticed the children helping each other when needed, and I believe all of this is because of my mentor teacher's hard work to keep her class organized and running smoothly.

Final Reflection

My two-week experience in Philadelphia was amazing, and I know this was mainly because of my mentor teacher. She was a phenomenal mentor, and I hope one day I will also be a great educator like her. I have been lucky to see a teacher who cares so much for her job and goes out of her way to buy and prepare materials for her classroom. Her preparation and hard work made her classroom management effective and she has enhanced the educational experience for all her urban students.

(Savanna Leninsky is a student at California University of PA.)

Reflections on a Tough Urban Classroom
Carrie Gutshall

Stepping into Mrs. G's classroom in downtown Philadelphia, my immediate response to her was excitement, as she was welcoming and eager to introduce me to her 3rd grade students. Her classroom has plenty of wall cubbies which are cheerfully decorated and prepared for 22 students, all of whom are Black or Hispanic. Mrs. G is not much taller than her students but she has a commanding presence in the classroom. She has been teaching here for nine years. Kindergarten has been her grade of choice until this year when she began teaching 3rd grade. The school building is old, but kept in good repair and seemingly functional, except for the "Don't Drink the Water" sign above the water fountains. The physical set up of the classroom is comparable to any other elementary class that I have visited in the past in rural or suburban school districts. None of this was surprising to me since I was expecting most of these elements to be the case.

However, I was surprised by the decibel level in the classroom. First, the students were all screaming over one another to be heard by a peer across the room. Backpacks were flying and chairs were screeching, all of which seemed to be normal for this class. Mrs. G contributed to the chaos with her screams of discontent. She tried to gain control by yelling, using clapping patterns, and threatening to call parents. Eventually, things calmed down after much time and effort to reel the students into her control.

As I began to get to know the students, Mrs. G asked me to teach a lesson. I was excited by her confidence in me but I felt unprepared. Mrs. G was testing each student individually and needed me to run the rest of the class. This was great, but I wish I could have changed and had a few minutes to go over what I was about to teach! I did not have time to read over the lesson book or think much about what I was going to teach or how I was going to teach it. Maybe Mrs. G wanted to see how I would respond to teaching on the fly without preparing for it.

My attitude was excitement, and I truly was excited! But I was also nervous. During the one lesson, she stopped me right at the beginning to describe what she wanted the students to take away from the lesson. I was thankful that she did, because I did not know to what they were supposed to be paying attention! This enabled me to direct my instruction toward the focal point of the lesson. I was thankful for her interruption but felt incompetent since Mrs. G had to stop the lesson to focus the lesson. I wish she would have clarified this before I started. But the rest of my teaching experience in the classroom went smoothly.

I was shocked by the degree of disrespect that was directed toward the teacher by the students. I was expecting this, but I was surprised by the intensity directed by the students. Any authority figure was vulnerable to attack. Students were explosive with their peers, too. They used aggressive, foul language and acted out violently. Mostly their aggression was taken out on inanimate objects like the water fountain or a desk, but I also witnessed students taking their frustrations out on the faces of their peers. All of these outbursts were sparked by seemingly small issues which made me realize that the actual point of origin for their disruptive behavior must come from outside of school since nothing that happened in the classroom justifies such rage.

Unique to urban classrooms, was the fact that negativity seemed to be an epidemic in inner-city schools. Teachers and parents alike seemed to have a rather biased attitude toward the students and often talked negatively about the children when the kids were standing right there. The kids did not seem to be disciplined with consequences. Instead they were constantly bombarded with orders and screaming. There was little, if any fun or affection going on in the classroom. This was sad considering that I believe that at their age, kids should have few worries in life and they should be able to relax and have fun. Instead, these children were stressed by their tense atmosphere and seemed always to be on edge in anticipation of the next negative comment to come their way. I think some positive interaction with students would have gone a long way in this situation. If kids know you care and you respect them, they will want to please you more than if you are just barking orders at them all day.

Also disheartening, was the lack of motivation by the kids to work hard and try harder. All the tickets and candy handed out to the students seemed to be unappreciated and irrelevant to the recipients. Some of the students even voiced their thoughts by saying, "I don't care. I can get that at the dollar store." Underneath, I am sure that the student does care but it is often a challenge for teachers to break through that hard, exterior shell to get to the soft heart inside. Inner drive is essential for these students to achieve their full potential. I believe this internal momentum starts at home with a positive connection to school and learning through reading books and writing the letters of the alphabet at an early age. Also, children will do as they see, so a good example from parents and teachers is vital. Self-determined motivation is essential for each student to reach their own success.

After taking in all that I saw, I began to ask myself many questions. First, I ask "why?" Why do they not want to excel in academics and what makes these young children so angry? Why is that one so sad? And why are they picking on the one in the black high tops? I do not have exact answers for ANY of these questions but after my first day, they are already keeping me up at night.

My next question that I ask is what can we do about it? What can be done about the stressors at home that these students face daily and carry heavily on their shoulders into class? And what can a school district do about the mother who does not bring her child into school until 11:00 am because she was out until 3:00 am the night before while her nine-year-old tried to wait up for her but crashed on the couch at 2:00 am?

I realize that there is a story behind each student, behind each face. Maybe the reason that the boy in seat 12 cannot focus today is because he did not have breakfast this morning, or dinner last night... Perhaps the scar on her forehead is from a fall down the stairs just as she explained or maybe not. Maybe the boy in the back with the dirty, stained clothes would feel better about himself and have a better day if his clothes were washed clean. And then there are the stains that cannot be washed out. The ones that leave scars on the inside that no one can see to minister to. There are no quick or easy answers to any of these questions.

But teachers can do something. We can seek ways to restore hope for the futures of these children as each one has a unique story and a specific need. Students need to know that they are safe at school physically and emotionally. Teachers can provide an accepting, nurturing environment while still setting distinct parameters in order to gain the respect and control of children in the classroom. Kids of all ages want and need boundaries. They need to be safe and they want to have a sense of predictability in their lives. Discipline, which provides a sense of security and structure in students' lives, is a positive characteristic of great teaching.

My most positive experience in working with the students was when Jessica, who is usually a great student, was reprimanded for chewing gum. Mrs. G was furious and really yelled at her. After leaving Jessica in the classroom and walking the rest of the class to lunch, I stayed behind with Jessica. I gave her a big hug. I supported Mrs. G by telling Jessica that she should not have gum in school and she knows better. I also told her that I understand why she was so upset and then I hugged her again. I walked her to the bathroom where I got her a cool paper towel and placed it on the back of her neck and forehead. She smiled, and said, "I bet you are a really good mom." This made my heart swell and I told her that I try to be. She never said, "thank you," but she did not have to. I knew it meant a lot to her that I was there to help her calm down and empathize with her feelings. I will never forget her face in that moment.

I believe that I did have stereotypes before this experience. I thought these kids were harsh with hard shells. I learned that some of them are. But all of them have a soft interior once you got past the outside front. These kids are like all other kids all over my rural neighborhood. They like to play jump rope and play clapping games. They love to laugh and they do want to please you. These inner-city students appreciate your smile and your compassion just as any other kid does anywhere. And the best part is that I think the inner-city kids appreciate it more. Maybe some of them do not get as much love or affection at home or at school compared to the kids in my neighborhood at home. This makes them thirsty for any kind of reassurance they can get! I love this about them. They never under appreciate any effort made to help them feel better or make them smile.

During this experience, I have realized that students in urban areas are more similar to students in rural areas than they are different. They all have a need for compassion and attention, and a passion for knowledge. Kids should not be classified by their circumstances but by how they achieve success. I have discovered that I really loved working with these kids and if I was single with no children, I would seriously consider working in such a school. I was surprised by this. I thought for sure this course was just a way to earn three credits quickly, but those students were hard to walk away from. I would love to work with these students if my circumstances were different. Also, I have a great confidence now that I am a compassionate and sympathetic person. I know that when I am a teacher, I will not forget these urban students and I will be ready for any student coming into my classroom who may have a similar background. I feel confident that I will know how to approach and reach each child in a manner that works for them.

The most important realization I have discovered during this urban experience is that while we may want to scoop up all the kids we can hold and carry them home to show them what it is to be loved and what a healthy family life is supposed to look like, we cannot. Rescuing them from some of their situations is not the answer. It is vital to help improve the lives of these kids, but they need to rise above their own misfortune. They need to know that there is love, support, and hope outside of the turmoil of their everyday lives. When students realize this on their own, with the support of caring teachers and positive role models, they can choose to change their own lives. Once this choice is made, there is no end to what a redeemed child can accomplish. In the mean time while children are still acquiring their own sense of self-determination for success, teachers must raise up their students when they cannot elevate themselves. As educators and positive role models for underprivileged students, it is necessary that we constantly love and support them along their journeys, as they have a brutal and exhausting path ahead. With the right motivation, nourishment, and discipline any student can be a successful learner.

(Carrie Gutshall is a student at Shippensburg University.)

Understanding Our Students Leads to Effective Teaching
Valerie Phipps

With only one semester of classes remaining before I was to begin student teaching, I felt that the Philadelphia Urban Seminar would be a beneficial opportunity for me. I was hoping to benefit from a full day classroom experience because my previous field experiences had been for brief blocks of time. The classroom experience in Philadelphia far exceeded my expectations. I learned much about myself and about the importance of understanding the behaviors of the students in my classroom.

My training, from the Special Education Department at California University of Pennsylvania, is behaviorist based. I have been taught that students' behavior is being reinforced by their environment. My experience in the School District of Philadelphia has shown me that while many times student behavior is linked to reinforcers within the classroom, it may also be linked to external factors that cannot be influenced by their teacher. There are situations that occur outside of the school environment that control student behavior. The most important thing that I learned during my time in Philadelphia is that inner-city teachers must discover the individual needs of students and find a way to best accommodate each student in the classroom. It is like waitressing; you must make every "customer" feel as if they are the only one who matters; the only one "eating in the restaurant." This realization was discovered over the two week session; it did not happen in one day.

While conducting my observations in the classroom during the first few days of the Urban Seminar, I noticed that one of the students was off-task for the majority of the day. There were extended periods of time when she would sleep on her desk. I went over to her desk to wake her up and ask if she was feeling alright, her response was that she was tired because she was up late with her baby sister. During the preparation period, I talked to my cooperating teacher about the situation. She told me that this is not a surprise. She stated that she receives text messages from this particular student at 3:30 AM. She also stated that the student shares a room with her baby sister who was born in November. The student's home is occupied by the student, her mother and approximately 13 other minors including siblings, cousins and significant others. Because of these conditions, the student often sleeps during the morning classes because she does not get sufficient rest at home. After lunch and recess, she is generally more alert. The problem for her is that most of the academic lessons are conducted in the morning, and the afternoon consists of mostly independent work.

I felt that I needed to do something to help this student prepare for her math exam that was coming soon. During the independent reading time one afternoon, I asked her to come into the hall with me. We sat in the hall, and I retaught the math lesson that was taught to the class that morning. The student was very motivated and enthusiastic about participating in the "mini lesson." She was gracious and thanked me repeatedly for helping her. I thought I had really done something good. The problem arose the next morning when I noticed the same student was sleeping during math class again. She refused to stay awake, and simply said she was too tired. She asked if I could just help her after lunch again. I did not know what to do. Had I done the wrong thing by pulling her out of class? I asked the classroom teacher, and she said no, it was not acceptable for her to choose to sleep through class, but that it had been helpful for me to pull her out the day before.

I spent the majority of the day trying to keep the student awake and focused on the lessons that were being taught to the full class. She rarely listened to what was being said, and when she was listening, she did not complete her assignments. The classroom teacher insisted that she, and one other student who was sleeping, stand for the remaining portion of the lesson. She explained to me after class that she had to do something because other students were asking her why those two were allowed to sleep, why they were able to do anything they wanted to do.

Many of the other students in the classroom have noticeable, specific academic and emotional needs. These needs are present in every classroom; the range of needs is simply greater in the urban setting. It is the responsibility of the teacher to identify the needs of each student in his or her class and then find some way to provide the necessary accommodations. These accommodations can range from providing high levels of verbal praise and attention during lessons to individualized instruction and assistance during independent tasks. While the classroom teacher makes efforts to ensure that each student feels as if they are the only student in the classroom, it is crucial that students do not begin to feel as if the teacher has a favorite. As soon as students ask why one of their classmates is receiving special treatment, the teacher knows that the accommodations that are being made are not appropriate. This is something that I witnessed during my experience with the Urban Seminar.

My cooperating teacher was allowing the student I talked about at the beginning of this article to sleep because it was obvious that rest was a necessity for her. This was not a problem in the classroom until the other students started asking why this particular student was allowed to sleep and not do her work. One student said that because she was sleeping, he also went to sleep on his desk. This is when my cooperating teacher decided that accommodating the needs of a single student is not as important as conducting the classroom in a manner that is beneficial to the majority of the students in the class. When the behavior of one student is negatively impacting the education of the rest of the class, something has to be done. Although when she was told she could not sleep, the student refused to participate in the lesson, this was not making any negative impact on her education personally because she was not benefiting from the lessons when she was asleep anyway. However, when the two students were told they could not sleep, both the boy and the rest of the class became more focused on the lessons that were being presented by my cooperating teacher.

I had the opportunity to spend some time bonding with this young girl one-on-one during the preparation period one day. She had begged my cooperating teacher to spend the prep period with us instead of going to science. The teacher allowed this because of the student's situation and because the science teacher had a review planned rather than a new activity or lesson. While spending time with me the student opened up to me without my asking. She talked about her feelings about school, her home life and what she thinks of my cooperating teacher. We were walking through the halls and she turned to me and said, "You know what I love most about the teacher? She understands me." After that statement the young girl went on to tell me how important it is to her that my cooperating teacher understands that she needs attention, and sometimes cannot control her behavior. She told me about the many experiences that she and my cooperating teacher have had, the ways that they have grown close over the year and how the other students see her because of the relationship. My cooperating teacher has reached out to this young girl many times on a personal level, going as far as taking her out to dinner twice. This personal connection has inspired the student to willingly do as my cooperating teacher asks more often. Sometimes other students get mad and tell this student that she can do anything she wants and that she will not get in trouble. This bothers her because she is not accepted by her peers, but she still appreciates the attention that is provided to her by my cooperating teacher. She explained to me that at home she does not get much attention from her mom because she has seven children, one being only five months old.

My experience with the young girl and my cooperating teacher through the Urban Seminar has taught me the significance of understanding our students and building relationships with them. I witnessed, first-hand, how influential a teacher can be in a student's personal life. This personal relationship between student and teacher then turns around and positively impacts the student's academic performance. If a student feels unwelcome or useless, they are not going to participate in educational activities. When a teacher appeals to a student's emotions, he or she is able to connect with the student on a whole new level.

My cooperating teacher maintains an authority position in the classroom. She makes sure that her students are aware that she really does care about them and that she is teaching them for their own benefit. I have heard stories from both the young student, and my cooperating teacher, about the young girl's life, and they are heart wrenching. These stories are the reason why students like her need a strong support system at school. She does not have access to a sufficient support system when she is at home.

The understanding and cooperation that a teacher establishes in the classroom with the students encourages student participation and success. Students are more likely to cooperate with an adult who cares about them, understands them and is willing to work with them. As teachers, we should not be heartless and completely rule-oriented. We have to listen to our hearts, and show the students that we care, and give them an opportunity to show us who they are. Mutual respect and understanding between teachers and students leads to productive, academically oriented, and emotionally supportive classrooms. Although there are sometimes reinforcers maintaining behavior outside of the school building, there is always something that the teacher is capable of changing in the classroom to encourage appropriate behavior from the students.

(Valerie Phipps is a student at California University of PA.)

Saying Goodbye
Eliza Altenderfer

Although there are many things about Philadelphia that were incredibly memorable to me, there was one boy in my class whom I will never, ever forget. We will call him Jamal, for the sake of the story. Jamal was one of the smaller boys in class and did not entirely fit in—he had a severe learning and developmental disability that made him look physically different to the point where his eyes actually appeared to bulge out of his head. He rarely spoke but when he did, it was in a slow, soft, gravelly tone more suited to an old man than an eleven-year-old boy.

I found out that Jamal was one of twelve children, and mom had another one on the way—no dad in the picture, though. His developmental therapist would come to class and even go to his home to try to work with him, but with twelve other siblings, Jamal's problems were not at the top of any list. The neglect that he suffered did not just show in his behavior, it showed physically as well—his clothing was usually wrinkled and visibly dirty.

The school that I was placed at had a school wide science fair coming up, so Mrs. K, the teacher in the classroom where I was placed gave her students time to work on their projects in class. Most of the students were fairly self-sufficient, so I was left with nothing to do except organizing some of the tracing letters that Mrs. K prepared for her students. As some of the boys finished their projects, they slowly gravitated towards my table at the back of the room. We started talking as they helped me sort out the letters, and ended up discussing all sorts of things—what they wanted to be when they grew up, their favorite parts of school, and even the idea of speaking multiple languages. They started questioning me as to whether I spoke another language, and were amazed by the fact that I spoke Spanish. They had to test me of course (the school was in a predominantly Puerto Rican neighborhood so many of the students were bilingual), but were dumbstruck by my ability to understand and respond to them in their native language.

They were also fascinated by my knowledge of American Sign Language although I only know basic conversational phrases and the alphabet, they were enthralled. They all wanted to learn, but particularly (and most surprisingly) Jamal. I taught them the alphabet and worked on spelling a few words with them before it was time to go. They honestly did not learn much, but they seemed to enjoy their newfound knowledge of how to say "Hi, my name is…" and simple words like "apple."

The next day, Mrs. K confronted me, asking me what I had taught the boys the day before when they were back at the table with me. Immediately assuming the worst (how much trouble can a fifth grade boy create with the alphabet in sign language?), I managed to stammer "Just a few phrases, things like 'Hi, my name is…,' and I taught them the word 'apple.'" "Why? What happened?" Mrs. K simply asked me to show her what the word "apple" looked like—of course I obliged. She gazed at me for a moment, and then told me that Jamal had been repeating that over and over while waiting in the line to go home the day before. I made a point to watch him that day as well, and noticed that he would sit in class with his hand moving through the alphabet when he thought that no one was looking.

My two weeks sped by and before I knew it, it was my last day in the schools—and time to say goodbye. The goodbyes were sincere and bittersweet from all of the students. Many of the boys considered themselves too macho to say goodbye, but the girls sent me on my way with little notes ("Miss A you are the best teacher ever! I thank God for sending you to us. I love you. P.S. Your really pretty [sic]") and as much of a hug as they could give me from sitting down, since Mrs. K was in a time crunch and could not give them time to say goodbye however they would have wanted. Some of them broke the unspoken rule of no hugs—either by almost tackling me in the playground as one little girl did every morning, or by asking to go to the bathroom when it was time for me to leave. They found their ways to say goodbye, and each seemed more poignant than the last.

The sadness worn plain upon their faces was enough to break your heart—even I, a usually stoic sort, was close to tears. The worst goodbye, however, was the one that came from Jamal. When the rest of the class was lining up to leave the room he walked over to me nervously. I asked him what he needed and when he looked up at me, he was visibly upset. "Miss A," he started, "Why do you have to leave? Don't you want us no more?" Suddenly, every excuse that I had been giving about why I had to leave—I had a summer job, the program was only two weeks—seemed feebly pathetic and absolutely inconsequential. Some of the children in the school, who previously had few people who cared about them, had been sent to us potential teachers who were excited to be in the classrooms and willing to care about the students, but I am leaving again. All these seemed almost a cruel joke: giving them one more person who cared once but ultimately left once again.

These students need teachers who care—teachers who are committed to their students and who are not just in it for the paycheck. Letting a student give you a hug, playing handball with them at recess, and talking to them about their dreams… These smallest things can mean so much to them. It really is true—sometimes a smile can make a world of difference.

(Eliza Altenderfer is a student at Pennsylvania State University.)

Chapter Three

Learning the City of Brotherly Love

An important part of preparing students to teach in an urban setting is helping them appreciate the opportunities that cities offer. In this chapter, authors describe how they came to learn about and appreciate various cultural treasures that are found in Philadelphia.

Many people have noted that it is not buildings, statues, museums, or sports that make cities great. It is the people who live there that give a city its life. Professor Geraldine Jenny confirms this as she describes some of the people she met in Philadelphia and how those people made a lasting impression on her.

Kristen McCoy reminds us that it is the children in our cities that need teachers who will understand them and be able to teach them to reach for the stars. In order to do this, she realizes that we must break the stereotypes that are associated with urban life.

A real benefit of living and working in a city is the ethnic diversity that most large cities offer. Philadelphia is no exception. Jessica Barker relates an unexpected and delightful experience that she and her friends enjoyed one night in Philadelphia's China Town.

Not everything about living in the city is wonderful. Amy Leverentz recalls some of the hardships that are often a consequence of living in some of the old buildings in the city. Yet, despite those hardships, she also recalls how friends and others helped her cope with what, in retrospect, were the kinds of inconveniences that many people face every day.

Although cities can offer challenges, they also often provide incredible resources. Austin Cromartie describes how he learned of the many resources for personal enrichment and for teaching that are available from the Philadelphia Museum of Art, the scene of Rocky Balboa's triumphal ascent of the entry steps.

This chapter concludes with David Livengood's whimsical adaptation of Dr. Seuss' "Oh, the place you'll go!" In his poem, Professor Livengood describes many of the joys and challenges that are experienced by all participants in the Philadelphia Urban Seminar.

Memorable Philadelphians
Geraldine C. Jenny

As a citizen of the world, I have taken my responsibilities very seriously to see as much of that world as possible. I have been privileged to see Mayan ruins in Mexico, magnificent cathedrals in Spain, archaic fishing villages in Portugal, lavender English moors and majestic Scottish Highlands as well as breathtaking panoramas in the Caribbean.

And yet, as I reminisce about my travels, it is not the awe inspiring scenery that remains in my mind's eye. It has been the people that I have met along the way that live in my heart... An Irishman hobbling along a Dingle Peninsula country road and making the effort to speak to me for an incredible half hour in his native Gaelic... A Spanish shepherd who honored me with an invitation into his humble home to share homemade goat's milk cheese that he would otherwise have sold at market to feed his family... A Portuguese shopkeeper who promptly closed his store to lead our vehicle to a distant mountain destination located several hours away... A Turkish Muslim who served a feast to honor and share his cultural heritage and beliefs.

Not surprisingly, when I think about the annual Philadelphia Urban Seminar, it is not the Liberty Bell, Independence Hall or the Constitution Center that comes to mind, it is the people of Philadelphia who have inspired me and now live alongside the international residents of my heart. Each spring for the past five years, I have been accompanying approximately 20 Slippery Rock University (SRU) students to teach in inner-city classrooms of the "City of Brotherly Love." Perhaps this original moniker is not considered relevant in these modern times in a society that has become increasingly self absorbed. However, I have learned that brotherly love is indeed thriving to such a degree that original residents William Penn or Ben Franklin would still have ample reason to be proud of their historic city.

To illustrate my point, I will share a few portraits of inspirational Philadelphians I have met during the Urban Seminar. Looking back, I certainly had mixed feelings before going to the big city. Being a small town resident, I was leery before going to Philadelphia about whether the inhabitants of such a large city would be friendly or whether we might become victims of some terrible crime. However, in the past five years of living in the city, I have learned the error of my previous beliefs about city dwellers.

The first year that I attended the Urban Seminar, my adventurous students were looking for something different to do on a Friday night. A colleague suggested that we take a side trip to the quaint suburb of Manayunk. So with a dozen students in tow, we ventured out. When we reached Manayunk, we looked around for ways to spend our evening.

Surprisingly, we found ourselves wandering into the local fire station where we were greeted heartily by the Fire Chief and several volunteer firemen. They enthusiastically demonstrated the firefighting equipment and sounded the shrieking siren for us. As inquisitive future teachers, my students loved climbing all over the gleaming fire truck and trying on the firemen's boots, hats and jackets. We had such fun and were extremely impressed with the friendly firemen of Manayunk.

The students and I meandered down the street to a little ice cream shop on the main drag. We were warmly welcomed by "Jim" the owner. He volunteered to take us on a night tour of the town and immediately locked up his shop for some moonlight exploring. We began by walking on a railroad trestle that runs over a canal beside the town. It was amazingly frightening, but exhilarating to creep along the tracks with the river rushing below us. From there, our guide sat with us under an old oak tree and enlivened us with ghost stories of former townspeople as well as local legends about the town origins. Jim culminated that segment of our tour by taking us to an abandoned warehouse where we scared ourselves silly as we creaked around the well worn floors and imagined workers of the last century.

It was getting late as we headed back to Jim's ice cream shop. Unbelievably, when we did, Jim drew the window shades, put a "closed" sign on his store and pulled out a bucket of plastic ice cream spoons. He invited my students to "Just go to it." We were told to sample any or all of the ice cream flavors to our hearts' content. Whenever we tried a new flavor, we used a new spoon to keep the ice cream pails pristine. We felt as if we were in hog heaven as we each gorged ourselves courtesy of our generous host. What an eventful evening was provided by a remarkable man to these future teachers. Jim taught all of us an unforgettable lesson in hospitality and human kindness that my students and I are still talking about.

The purpose of the Urban Seminar is for college students to experience inner-city classrooms with students of diverse cultures. One of my responsibilities as their supervisor is to visit the schools to which they have been assigned and thank their principals for hosting them in the schools. On a bright May morning, I drove to a dilapidated old stone multi-story school and met a building principal whose passion for kids is unparalleled. After brief introductions, Dr. Barsky ushered me into his office where I was invited to sit down as he took the time to explain why he chose to stay in the same Philadelphia neighborhood where he grew up and work at the same school that he had attended.

As Dr. Barsky spoke, the enthusiasm and love for his students and their families shone in his eyes. He prided himself in maintaining open communication and partnering with the families to whom he was so dedicated. I quickly learned that he was a principal who had had many opportunities to leave the city and advance his career in what many would consider easier surroundings. However, in following his heart and staying in the neighborhood with the people he loved, he motivated his students to achieve far more than is anticipated and predicted for urban youth.

I met my third notable Philadelphian while waiting in the SRU van for my Urban Seminar students to finish one day. During my wait, I became fascinated by an African American woman wearing a floppy straw hat who was carefully thinning and transplanting Hosta in the street's median strip. Curious, I rolled down my window and complimented the lady on her gardening skills. She introduced herself as "Miss Phyllis" and shared with me that she had lived in her neighborhood since the 1930's and had taken it upon herself many years ago to be a caretaker and beautify the area. Through perseverance and many tedious hours, this has been accomplished without any help or donations from others. Miss Phyllis explained that she even hooks up her garden hose to her own kitchen faucet to water the beautiful flowers, plants and shrubs she is growing in this authentic labor of love. Previously, my students and I had envisioned the inner city to be a place of overflowing garbage and graffiti evidencing very little pride of ownership. But Miss Phyllis showed us that cultivating an appreciation of one's surroundings may be lovingly nurtured— even in places classified as "poverty stricken." The SRU students and I repeatedly witnessed pride of ownership in neighborhoods of diverse cultures.

I eagerly anticipate returning this spring with my Urban Seminar students to the streets of Philadelphia and the people who call the "city of brotherly love" their home. In five years of annual pilgrimages there, my earlier beliefs have only been confirmed regarding the importance of being open-minded enough to learn the individual residents of a place in order to fully appreciate it.

(Geraldine C. Jenny is an assistant professor at Slippery Rock University.)

My Time in the City
Kristen McCoy

The Urban Seminar is the most rewarding experience that I have been able to participate in during my three years at West Chester University. During October of my sophomore year, I heard about the Urban Seminar and added the Seminar to my list of "must do's" before I graduate in the fall of 2010. A student who participated in the Seminar told me that it was the first time that she actually felt like a teacher because she was in the classroom, all day, for two straight weeks. Another student said, "I wanted to try a new teaching in a new area so I chose to participate in the Seminar. I never thought I would love teaching in Philadelphia as much as I did. It was the most inspirational experience I have ever had." After hearing such great personal experiences from other West Chester students I decided I would participate in the experience, too. During the final weeks for the spring semester, meetings were held to discuss the details of the Seminar. After picking roommates and making lists of necessities that come along with dorm life, nerves started to kick in. I was worried about what the dorms would be like, what school I would be placed in, if any other West Chester students would be in my group, and if I was ready to be in the classroom for two whole weeks. The morning of May 17th finally came and everyone met at Central High School located on West Olney Avenue, in the Northwest Region of the school district. We split up into university groups and listened to opening remarks from many different educators. Later that afternoon, we moved into the dorms at La Salle University which were large and spacious but not very clean. Some dorm rooms had cockroaches and mice.

The first night a few girls from West Chester and I were talking about how this seminar was going to make or break our decision to teach in the City of Philadelphia or another urban setting.

On day one, Jen, another student from West Chester, and I found our van and started our journey to school. There were eleven girls in our van, going to two different elementary schools. After dropping off three students at the first school, I became increasingly more nervous to arrive at my school. When we arrived at our school we were welcomed by the principal and other staff members. We were then given a tour of the school and the annex. The annex was separate from the school and the kindergarten and first grade classrooms are held here. I was shown to Room 8, Mrs. Brick's classroom and this was where I would spend the next two weeks. The classroom was large and filled with many different activities for the students to get involved in. Mrs. Brick has five book shelves with different activities and games for her students to play. She also has a closet full of books and reading activities.

Mrs. Brick is a kindergarten and first grade resource room teacher and has fifteen different students at different times during the day. Most of the students come in two times throughout the day, once in the morning for reading and then in the afternoon they came for mathematics. Mrs. Brick told her students that I would be coming to spend two weeks in their classroom and they were very excited. The students asked many questions about what I would do, what I would look like, and if I would be there every day. All of the students wanted to know who I was and where I was from. They were very interested in having another teacher in their classroom.

On the first day, in Room 8, three students stood out. Two of the students were Alejandro and Cassandra, who were twins in kindergarten. English was their second language, and they were both diagnosed with learning disabilities in math and reading. Alejandro and Cassandra came from a Spanish speaking household. The third student that stuck out to me was Mikal, who was a first grade student in Room 9. He was "that kid I would know by the end of the week!" Mrs. Brick told me three different stories about Mikal on the first day. After meeting these three students, I knew that students like these were why I wanted to be a teacher and why I want to teach in Philadelphia.

Alejandro and Cassandra walked into the classroom and sat down at different tables from each other, Cassandra finished her breakfast and cleaned up quickly while Alejandro took his time and did not worry about getting ready for class. Mrs. Brick and I were talking and she told me that while they were twins, Alejandro and Cassandra were very different but similar at the same time. Cassandra was very open and talkative while Alejandro was not as talkative and more reserved.

Cassandra and Alejandro learned English as a second language. Even though they learned English after they learned Spanish, they both speak very well. In the classroom, they both showed initiative to learn and they wanted to do well. Cassandra always answers questions and made sure she understood the concepts we were learning. Alejandro was less noticeable but always asked individual questions to Mrs. Brick. Mrs. Brick did everything she could in order to help them be the best they could be.

The ambition and motivation that Cassandra and Alejandro showed in the classroom was incredible to see. Every day when they were in the classroom, these two asked questions and answered Mrs. Brick's questions. During lessons, Cassandra and Alejandro sit in their seats and listened attentively to Mrs. Brick. They kept their eyes on her and were intrigued by what she is saying. Outside of school Cassandra and Alejandro had many family problems. They would tell Mrs. Brick that their mom did not come home the night before and that they had to wear the same clothes from the day before. One day at the end of class, Alejandro came up to Mrs. Brick and told her that he had not seen his dad in three days and his mom said they did not have any money. Mrs. Brick comforted him by letting him know she would try to talk to his family and that he could come to her whenever he needed her. Their mother and father did not speak very much English which hindered Cassandra and Alejandro in school because they only spoke Spanish at home. While they were at school, their mother was at home and their father was at work. The family did not have a lot of money and the students wore the same uniform for three or four days in a row. Cassandra came in with the same ketchup stains on her collared shirt four days in the same week. In spite of many family problems and other things going on in their lives, they always came to school ready to learn and get things done.

During my stay in Philadelphia, I became very ill and had to make a doctor's appointment. I found a doctor that would take my insurance but could not get an appointment for three days. On the day of my appointment, I left school early and drove to the doctor. Once I found the parking garage, it took me ten minutes to find a parking spot and another ten minutes to find the building I was going too. I took an elevator to the fourth floor of the building and walked in three offices before I found the receptionist. After I arrived at the receptionist, I told her my name and she told me that my appointment was for the day before. I became extremely frustrated and asked, the women behind the desk, what I was supposed to do next. She walked away from the desk and asked me to, "Wait one minute." When she came back, she told me that they could fit me in that day. I waited for forty-five minutes and when I finally saw the doctor she told me that I was sick. I asked her what I should do and she told me that I should get rest and I would be okay. When I left the doctor's office, I was extremely angry. I did not believe that it was so difficult for me to get an appointment, find the office, and get an answer from the doctor. I am a Caucasian middle class woman whose first language is English. This experience was something that I am glad I went though. Now, I can try to imagine how hard it would be for a Spanish speaking family to do the same thing.

Back at school, Mikal, from room 9, was "that kid" I was going to know by the end of my two weeks. He was in a first grade classroom across the hall. Mr. Mike was his one-on-one to help with behavior support. The first day at our school, Mikal was singing at the top of his lungs and dancing through the hallways. Later in the day, Mrs. Brick and I were sitting at lunch and she told me a story about three interesting occurrences with Mikal.

Within three weeks, Mikal had been suspended from school for ten days. At the beginning of the first week Mikal found the leg of a desk at his house. He put the leg in his backpack and brought it to school. During first period, he took the desk leg out of his backpack and told two little boys that he was going to "Beat the living shit" out of them. He started to swing the desk leg at them but a teacher grabbed it before he could hit the students. Mikal was then taken to the office of the vice-principal who could not believe that a student would bring a desk leg to school and try to harm another student with it. Mikal was then suspended for the rest of the day and the next day.

The day after Mikal was able to come back to school, he was having a great day. After the students came back from lunch, Mikal went into his backpack and took out three needles. The needles were rusty, filthy, and looked as if they had been used. Mikal took the needles out of his bag and put them on a nearby desk. He was about to stab another student in the arm when Mr. Mike noticed that what was happening. He yelled, "Mikal! What are you doing?!?!?!" Mikal turned to Mr. Mike, still holding the needle, and said, "Giving George a shot." Mr. Mike pulled the needles off the desk and threw them into a bag. Mikal was then suspended for four days for bringing a dangerous object to school.

Just over a week since his last suspension, Mikal's teacher, Mrs. Smith, was absent. Mikal did not do well with substitutes and Mr. Mike had to work with two other students. Under these circumstances, Mikal was allowed to spend the day in Mrs. Brick's room. He was told he needed to sit quietly and do the activities with the other students and if he did then he could have time on the computer. All morning Mikal did everything Mrs. Brick asked him to do. When the students came back after lunch, he was able to play on the computer for having a great morning. Five minutes before the end of the day Mrs. Brick sent Mikal back to Mrs.

Smith's classroom because she needed to get her things together and do bus duty. When Mikal went into his classroom to get his backpack and sit at his desk, he sat down and pulled out a large kitchen knife. The substitute took the knife from Mikal and placed it up high. She asked Mr. Mike to get the vice-principal because she did not know what to do. The vice-principal walked Mikal out to meet his father in the yard and told him what had occurred and that he would be suspended for five days.

After Mrs. Brick told me these stories, I went back into the classroom and introduced myself to Mikal and immediately became curious as to why he acted the way he did. I wanted to know more about Mikal and the reasons behind his behavior. Mikal seems to react well to Mrs. Brick and I believe that she would be able to figure out some of the reasons behind the behaviors. Mikal made me want to be the one he could come talk to, so I could help him through his problems. I could not help but think there must be more that we could do to help Mikal and that suspension was not the answer.

Cassandra, Alejandro, and Mikal reinforced two of the major reasons of why I want to be a teacher. They reminded me that all children need someone that will understand them and be able to teach to reach for the stars, including children from urban settings. These students are capable of going far in their lives and breaking out of the stereotype of being from the inner-city. I want to be that teacher who helps students recognize their potential and teaches them how to reach their potential.

(Kristen McCoy is a student at West Chester University.)

An Unexpected Visit in China Town
Jessica Barker

Our last day in Philadelphia was quickly approaching and we had really been wanting to go to China Town. It was me and two other girls and a white mini-van with a state license plate. It was around dusk so we were a little nervous to be wandering the streets in the dark, but we figured that we would be okay as long as we stayed on main streets and stayed together.

We lapped China Town about seven or eight times before finding a parking space about two blocks outside of town. We walked into town and were so excited to see all of the Chinese inspired architecture and food and hear all of the different styles of music from store to store. Several Chinese groceries were first on our list and the three of us were amazed at all of the foods we saw that were so different from our culture; we each found something that interested us and bought it for the next day's snack.

Some firemen were sitting outside of the firehouse and asked us where we were from. We got to talking with them about where we were each from and what we were doing in Philadelphia. They had not heard of the Philadelphia Urban Seminar, which surprised me since it had been going on for so many years, I would have thought that they would have spoken to some students that had been on the experience before.

While we were standing and talking with the firemen, there was a lot of loud drumming going on. I was curious as to where it was coming from and when I asked, one of the firemen told me it was the dragon dancers practicing. He followed up by asking if we would like to see them practice and of course we were excited to watch. I was little hesitant because I had been warned several times about going anywhere with people I did not know and, while this man was a fireman, anyone can be a murderer. The three of us girls looked at each other and I could tell they were a little hesitant as well, but we decided to go for it anyway because there was one of him and three of us and the other firemen knew where he was taking us.

Across the street and down an alley is where he led us and I was getting a little nervous. On the way, he pointed out a brothel which lightened up the mood a bit. One of the other girls asked him why they did not do anything about it if they knew what was going on and he said that it was because it was their way of life.

They were not harming anyone and no one was harming them and there were many bigger problems to worry about. The fireman also pointed out a couple of people gambling that we could see in a window. He said that as long as it remained peaceful, they would let it continue.

Two doors down was the door he took us inside. Up three floors we hiked and I could hear the drums getting louder and louder causing my excitement to grow. We reached the floor that we needed to and went inside and everyone there knew the fireman. The room was all open and there were decorative ornaments everywhere. There were swords and knives, outfits, trophies, statues of all size, even a small pond; I could have looked around the room for days. He asked the dancers if they minded if we watched and not one minded a bit. They performed a few songs for us and two men danced with knives, it was incredible to see so close! I had only ever seen anything like this on television. The look on our three faces must have been astonished because we could not close our mouths or blink our eyes.

The group of us stayed up to watch for about twenty minutes before we decided to head back down. We were so thankful of this fireman to take us to see this practice. After we got back to the firehouse, the other firemen asked how we liked it and we could not stop talking about it for several minutes. We were getting pretty hungry, so we asked where they suggested to eat. There was a restaurant across the street called the Lotus that they told us to go to and they told us to tell them that we knew the firemen, but before we went to eat, they asked what state our license plate had and we told them Pennsylvania. They were glad we had a Pennsylvania license plate and told us that sometimes the homeless people will break in the windows of out of state license plates. They do it because the out of state residents usually end up dropping charges before anything happens because you have to be in the state of the crime to do anything about it and this way the homeless people never get in trouble. Their reason for doing it though I am not sure.

Next they asked where we were parked. The van was parked a few blocks away, so they told us to go and get it and park at the firehouse so we did not have to walk so far once it was late. It was so nice of them to let us do this and we were completely taken off guard when they told us to do it. We were nervous about walking the streets at night, so of course we did what they said. When we got back with the van they moved all of their chairs to let us pull in.

Across the street we headed once we knew the van was safe, we were so excited for some China Town Chinese food. The food was delicious and it was difficult to finish the large servings. After the great food, we headed back to the firehouse to get the van and head home, but we ended up getting held up a little longer. One of the girls was a huge Penguins hockey fan and there happened to be a game on. She asked if they knew the score and they invited us into the firehouse to watch the end since it was about over.

On the way in, I noticed one of the firemen talking to a lady on the bench outside. She looked like she might be homeless but he seemed to know her. We went inside and watched some of the game and then the man that was talking to the lady outside told us to give her a soft pretzel. Not sure if he was serious we all just stared at him. He said, "I'm serious, who wants to go and give this to her?" So we all went out and gave her the pretzel. She looked surprised but was very happy, she did not speak much English, but we could tell by her expression that she appreciated it. The fireman said that they gave her food pretty often and most of them could speak Chinese to her from spending so much time with all of the China Town locals.

Our night was reaching an end and we knew we would have to get up early to teach the next day. We said our goodbyes and made our way towards the van. One of the firemen gave us directions for the easiest way to get back to LaSalle University. Once we were in the van, the firemen walked out into the street and blocked traffic so we could back out without any worries and we were on our way.

The night was incredible, one unexpected event led to the next. Everyone of the firemen we met was so friendly and helpful. They have the respect of the community as well as the three of us girls and I recommend anyone willing to go on an adventure to make a trip to the China Town fire house because they are certain to be amazed, not only by what they will see, but by the kind and welcoming attitudes of the firemen.

(Jessica Barker is a student at Indiana University of PA.)

My Adventure in the Dorm
Amy Leverentz

Before coming to Philadelphia, I tried to prepare myself for some of the new things I might see or hear. I told myself to remember that some of the students I may be working with come from very different backgrounds than I do and that I might see some behavior from the students that I had never seen in a classroom before. Some of the downtown buildings could be old and not as clean and as I hoped. I told myself that this experience was going to make me a better person because it will open my eyes to a larger world around me. Well, there are still things that I did not imaging far enough.

I am from a small town called Elizabethtown which is located in Lancaster County PA. I live in a residential neighborhood with my family in a nice, medium-sized home. Here, the streets are always pretty quiet. You do not hear sirens every five minutes and there are no cars flying down your street. Everybody knows their neighbors and kids are always running around in the backyards. I chose to leave all these behind for two weeks to experience a life completely different from what I was used to.

When we arrived at the inner-city Philadelphia I saw exactly what I had expected to see. There were many houses that seemed a little run-down and built right on top of each other. I knew that the living conditions in the city were going to be a little more difficult than my living conditions at home. I was amazed when we pulled up to La Salle University, however. The campus looked absolutely beautiful. I remember thinking, "Wow, I am really glad that we get to stay in such a nice place." I immediately began moving my things into my dorm room. I dragged my heavy suitcase into the elevator (which took a minute to shut because all of the girls there had brought suitcases just as big as mine) and rode it up to the second floor of St. Katherine's. I got off the elevator and made my way down the hall to the left to search for my room.

When I opened the door, I was a little disappointed. The beautiful campus had given me the impression that I was going to be staying in a very nice place; I really should learn not to judge a book by its cover. In our room, my roommate Michele and I, found two metal beds that appeared to me as though they had been constructed in about five minutes, two beat-up, brown desks complete with chairs that looked as though that had been used in school in the 1950's, two large, brown closets with three small drawers in them, dirty base-boards, a window that did not lock, an old refrigerator, a florescent light that ONLY hung above our closets (which means that Michele did not have any light over in her corner of the room because the closets were on my side of the room), and walls that were painted completely white so that you felt like you had to stay at the asylum. Yep, things were looking pretty different from home.

I was not really too worried about my room though. I had thought about the very large itinerary that we had received earlier that day and decided that it did not really matter much what my room looked like because I would not be spending a lot of time in there anyway. Michele and I then went down the hall to find out where the bathrooms were. It was like stepping into my room all over again. The bathroom sinks and mirrors looked as though they should have been replaced years ago, the toilet stalls needed a new paint job, you had to pee in the dark because there were not any lights placed over the stalls, the showers were dark as well because they also did not have any lights placed over them and they were very cramped with nowhere for you to change your clothes once you were finished. My first thought was, "Why on earth do these people pay $30,000 a year to go to college here when I pay less than half of that amount to go to a college with MUCH nicer living conditions?"

I was immediately appreciating the dorms at Shippensburg; and I was now a little homesick too. When Michele and I lay down to go to sleep that night, I turned off the lights and Michele said, "Oh my gosh! Someone wrote 'Murder You' on our ceiling!" I looked above her bed, and it did in fact say, "Murder You" in some kind of special glow-in-the-dark marker. I felt a little uneasy as I slipped off to sleep that night, but I just kept telling myself that I was only going to be living here for two weeks and that never hurt anybody.

As the days passed, Michele and I learned to get used to our new living conditions. We began to fall into a routine; we went to school all day, had an hour-long seminar at night, went to dinner, had a group discussion with the other Ship girls, talked to our families on the phone, and then went to bed. Throughout the week I remember hearing other students talking about rodent and bug problems. I had heard that there were some West Chester girls in another dorm room who had had their underwear chewed through by a mouse. I had also heard that some other students had seen cockroaches in their rooms as well. I was not surprised to hear these stories because I was already unimpressed by the living conditions.

It was not until Thursday night of the first week that I heard a girl down the hall scream because she had seen a cockroach. I had never seen a cockroach in my entire life. I walked down the hallway and, there it was, squished on the floor. I was pretty grossed out. I mean, I deal with bugs in my own house too but, not ones that were this big. I decided that, as long as I did not feel one crawling across my leg when I was sleeping, everything would be okay.

The next night was Friday night and our group had just come back from a very enjoyable night at Norris Square. We had been served some light appetizers there but I was craving some chocolate. I knelt down and pulled a duffel bag from under my bed in which I kept all my food. I began rummaging around in the bag for a snack when I noticed that one of my microwavable Raman Noodle cups had a hole in it. I set it aside; mentally scolding myself for originally shoving so much food in that bag that I must have put a hole in the Styrofoam cup. I continued rummaging and noticed that another one of my Raman Noodle cups also had a hole in it. I just stared at it. I remember that the initial thought that went through my head was, "These look like they have been chewed through." I immediately pushed this thought out of my head, however, and came up with a new one; "Oh, I just must have put a hole in this one too." I did not want to believe that, what I initially thought was happening, was actually happening.

When I pulled out the third Styrofoam cup, I realized that I had a mouse. To confirm my suspicions, I walked over to the girls in the room across the hall and showed them one of the cups. They said, "Looks like you have a little friend." I was so mad! I could not believe that this had happened to me! ME! Why me? I went back to my room and began taking all of the other food out of my bag and checking it to see if my "little friend" had gotten into anything else. Luckily, he had not. It appears that he only enjoys Raman Noodles (who doesn't).

At this point, one of the other girls, Meghan, came into my room and told me that I had better check my suit case as well; just to make sure he did not want a new pair of clothes too. I told Meghan that I could not deal with mice and I asked her if she would mind checking for me. She opened up my suitcase, moved my clothes around a bit and said, "I do not see any mouse, or any mouse poop so it looks like your suitcase is okay." I felt a little more relieved to hear this. I thought, "Okay, I can deal with this. After all, I only lost some 38-cent packs of Raman Noodles. I made off a lot better than the West Chester girls."

I took my bag to the bathroom and began wiping all of the Raman Noodle leftovers out of it. By now, all of the girls in the surrounding rooms had figured out what happened and they all began checking their food and suitcases to make sure that the mouse had not paid them a visit as well. I decided that I go through my suitcase again, just to be sure. It was then that I saw them; two little black poop turds… the mouse had penetrated my suitcase! I could not take it anymore; I started to cry. All I could think about was how much I hated it here; this was the only time that I had honestly just wanted to pack up my things and go home. At this point, my cell phone started ringing; it was Dad. I answered to phone but I was so upset that I could not even bring myself to say hello. Finally, I heard my dad, "Amy. Amy are you there?" All I could do was start crying into the phone. I briefly told him what had happened and then hung up the phone so that I could begin cleaning up the mess.

By now, almost all of my group members were huddled around my door, as well as, my professor, Dr. Bao, and a Residential Assistant at La Salle. The RA asked if he could get on my computer to fill out a maintenance request to get some mouse traps. I told him that he could as I began pulling clothes out of my suitcase to make sure that they had not been chewed through. Luckily, none of them had. The only present that the mouse had left me were a few poop turds and a nice big pee stain. I was so upset when I saw that pee stain. I thought to myself, "Oh great, I just ruined my grandparent's suitcase. That stain is never going to come out." Meanwhile, my phone was ringing again. This time, it was my boyfriend. He had called to see how my day was. I started crying again and told him that I would have to call him back later and tell him what had happened; I had to get everything cleaned up first.

Lucky for me, I came to this urban seminar with some very wonderful people. Everybody did what they could for me to try and help. Whitney went downstairs for me to get the RA; Dr. Bao helped to calm me down a bit by reminding me that I was not the only one who had had a problem like this and that these things happen. She gave me some "Wet-Wipes" to clean my suitcase. Austin wiped down my entire suitcase for me and worked very hard to get the pee stain out of it. Michele was there to comfort me and she helped me wash all of my clothes that had been in the suitcase. The next day, Dr. Bao took us to Wal-Mart to buy mouse repellent. Since none of us wanted to use the mouse trap for fear of that terrible squeaking sound if a mouse was trapped, she could only buy some mothballs to calm us down psychologically. Finally each of us bought a large plastic box so we can keep all our food and clothes in it.

Reflecting on the Urban Seminar I definitely learned a lot from this experience. I learned the hard way just how different urban life is from small town life. Inner-city life could be hard. Urban residents have to endure much more difficult conditions here than I have to living in my cozy house. Not only do they have to deal with lots of noise and urban poverty, but sometimes they have to deal with cockroaches and rodents. It truly makes me appreciate how I live at home. It also makes me realize what kinds of conditions that my students live in. They may not always live in a nice house with a green yard or sufficient heat. I will need to take these things into account when I am teaching and try to help provide some of the things that my students may not get enough at home.

I also learned a lot about the importance of friends. My friends helped me a lot throughout the Urban Seminar. They were there to help me when I had a problem and they were there to just listen to me when I wanted to talk. I realized that, without friends and family, life would not really be worth living. It is these people that can help you through the best of times and the worst of times. My friends and family are the most important people in the world to me and I am very appreciative of the love and support that they have given me.

I believe that the Urban Seminar has been a very good experience for me. I came into this wanting to come out a better person and I believe that I have achieved that goal. I have really been able to learn a lot about others through this program but, I have also been able to learn a lot about myself as well. I am very glad that I choose to participate in this program and it is definitely something that I will remember all my life.

(Amy Leverentz is a student at Shippensburg University.)

Learning in Philadelphia Art Museum
James Austin Cromartie

Philadelphia Art Museum is on the Urban Seminar's city tour repertoire, which was designed to expand worldly perceptions of seminar participants. The museum is situated at the end of the Benjamin Franklin Parkway. You can find its magnificent setting from a famous scene in the movie Rocky. As Sylvester Stallone embarks upon a vigorous training across the city for his big fight, he ends his run at a vast climb of stone steps. Charging up the steps, the Italian Stallion reaches the top and raises his arms, pumping his fists in triumph. A statue of this pose stands in the area, commemorating the beloved underdog character.

Now, many people know the story and most visitors and Urban Seminar participants cannot resist the urge to reenact this dramatic scene. So when you are satisfied with your victory gestures, you may turn around and bring your attention to the large building before you. That is the 125-year-old Philadelphia Museum of Art, one of the largest museums in the entire continental United States.

Allow your curiosity to draw you through the front entrance and into the cavernous main lobby. It is strangely quiet and serene as you gaze upon massive pillars looming tall beside you. The ceiling itself seems to graze the atmosphere and crowd the lower reaches of the heavens. The most noticeable object in the chamber is a large statue of a feminine figure drawing a bow and arrow.

The main building consists of three intricate floors of exhibits. A short, free trolley ride across the avenue will ferry you to the museum's second building, which was recently renovated. This is the Perelman Building and it houses an additional two floors of exhibits for your viewing pleasure. Aside from the sculptures and paintings, you will find more unconventional art displayed here like fashion and costumes.

Between the two structures, there are more than 200 galleries, over 2,000 years of artistic labor and 225,000 individual pieces of art. This is enough to turn even the most skeptical or disinterested viewer into an art lover. There are things for both the savvy and untrained eye alike to behold.

As you walk through the buildings, you will find works that range from paintings to sculptures, paperwork to metal piece, photography to furniture, textiles to decorations and from pottery to armor. The different halls are themed and encompass American Art, European Art, Asian Art, Arms and Armor, Modern and Contemporary Art, Prints, Drawings, Photographs and Special Exhibitions, which will vary depending on the time that you visit. During our visit, the current exhibition happened to be Cezanne and Beyond. These special exhibits, which rotate in and out of the Museum, required a timed ticket to view. So we did not get a chance to visit the special exhibits due to time constraint.

Upon entry into the Museum, I glimpsed something that snared my attention and carried me up the main staircase. Being a war history enthusiast, I marveled at the first exhibit I encountered. It was a fine collection of ancient weaponry and armor from Europe and parts of Asia. There were flintlock pistols, swords of every shape, halberds, spears, pikes, rifles, lances, shields, axes, helmets and full suits of armor. A subtle eerie feeling crept through me as I realized many of these instruments of combat were responsible for the early demise of many poor souls. Now I had lived in Europe for five years, and visited my fair share of museums. Therefore, I can say without a doubt, that the exquisite collection in Philadelphia rivals almost anything I had viewed overseas.

The grandest trick the Museum plays is the sensation that you have traveled back in time and fallen directly into a majestic foreign landscape. This feat is accomplished through the Museum's architectural settings. There are entire rooms from royal European estates to walk through, masterfully reconstructed, you practically forget that you are still inside the Museum. I also found myself brushing past actual bamboo plants and skirting the perimeter of a traditional Japanese teahouse. For a brief moment my mind left Pennsylvania and circled the globe. The authenticity and quality of the exhibits make them truly magical. Most relics and antiques are within reach but they are not allowed to be touched. The museum allows you to get quite close to all of its pieces but does stock each hall with a well-trained staff of security personnel, so be sure to respect the art, Museum and follow the rules.

Not only is the Museum a great source of artistic entertainment, but it also serves as an excellent foundation for educators. The ambition of the Museum is to direct students toward a greater comprehension and appreciation for art. In the Perelman Building, on the second floor, a utopia of knowledge awaits teachers.

The Wachovia Education Resource Center is a well-oiled machine operated largely by retired teacher and administrator volunteers. The foundation is designed to offer services to teachers free of charge, such as materials and lesson plans meant to develop art through an interdisciplinary curriculum. This drives students to obtain skills beyond simply accessing information, which the average mind can do quite easily in this day and age.

The volunteers upon email or phone request compile these materials, or when a teacher physically comes into the resource center. The teacher then is loaned the materials for a month at a time, things like DVDs, multimedia lessons, and color-coded subject folders. The Center's motto is, "After all, you're busy and we're free!"

Teachers have much more liberal restrictions in terms of copyrights than the general public, so it allows them to access to the greatest technological resource that the Center offers. The program is called ArtStore, an education database of high-resolution art images. One million images are at your fingertips and the ArtStore provides incredible magnification and refocusing ability for every image without pixel blurring. Lesson plans correspond with these images that make up PowerPoint type presentations.

The ArtStore also offers 360-degree virtual reality software for tours of actual historical landmarks and sites around the world. The teaching possibilities are endless and museum membership is not required to access the Wachovia Education Resource Center, but it is encouraged.

So if you are a student, parent or teacher, and you find yourself near Philadelphia, plan a trip to the Philadelphia Museum of Art. The experience will not disappoint you; it has certainly enriched artistic appreciation and world perspectives of Urban Seminar participants.

(James Austin Cromartie is a student at Shippensburg University.)

Oh! the Places We'll Go!
—An Urban Seminar Parody of Dr. Seuss' Poem "Oh! the Places You'll Go!"
David Livengood

Congratulations!
Today is our day.
We're off to Great Places?
We're off and away!

We have brains in our head.
And feet in our shoes.
The urban experience
Sends us in a direction we choose.

We are on our own. And we know what we know.
And we are the teachers who will know where to go.
We've looked up and down streets. Looked 'em over with care.
And about some we have said, "We don't want to go there."

With our heads full of brains and our shoes full of feet,
We're too smart to go down the one way street.

If we don't find a street
That we want to go down
If that is the case,
We know to head out of town.

We have learned things can happen
As all of us see.
To people as brainy
And footsy as we.

We know when things happen
We don't worry and stew.
We just go with the flow.
And we'll be happening too.

Wow!
The places we've been!
The things that we've learned!
The wonderful sights!
We'll join the great teachers
Who go to great heights.

The Urban Experience has provided the speed
We'll pass the whole gang and we will take the lead!

Wherever we go, we'll be the best of the best.
Wherever we go, we'll top all of the rest.

If you want to teach Urban
Today is your day!
Our cities are waiting.
So…get on your way.

Thank you Urban Seminar for all that we learned!
We are off to our future in the direction we've turned.

If we do not go Urban the time wasn't wasted or squandered,
We have learned about diversity as we have thought and pondered.

One way or another it was a time for powerful learning
When our minds were open and we were yearning.
For knowledge and experience that was needed
As we set our sights and our thoughts were seeded.

OH! THE PLACES WE'LL GO!

(David Livengood is an instructor at Bloomsburg University.)

Chapter Four

We Choose to Stay

A major problem faced by many inner-city schools in America is the high turnover rate among teachers, which adds considerably to the instability and lack of consistency that characterizes the lives of many urban children, especially those who grow up in poverty. One aim of the Philadelphia Urban Seminar is simultaneously expose pre-service teachers to both the challenges that often lead teachers to leave urban teaching, and to the opportunities that cities offer, in the hope that dedicated and effective teachers will choose to teach in urban settings, and once there, choose to stay.

This chapter contains articles written by former participants in the Philadelphia Urban Seminar who decided, upon completion of their university education, to teach in Philadelphia. In the opening article of this chapter, Kimberly Smith describes how she faced enormous obstacles in her first year of teaching in Philadelphia, but, despite those obstacles and challenges, made the deliberate choice to continue in Philadelphia as an urban teacher.

Shannon Taylor, also a teacher in Philadelphia and a former Urban Seminar participant, points out that when teaching in Philadelphia high-stress situations occur on a daily basis. However, she affirms that with calmness and flexibility, she has learned to handle those daily challenges, and, despite the reality of those challenges, she chose to stay.

Tysean Gross recalls his journey from being a student in the School District of Philadelphia, to being a pre-service teacher at Lincoln University, and finally ending up as a teacher in the very district where he grew up. Stephanie Montalvo describes how she starts out wishing to be a pediatrician but finds great fulfillment teaching in an inner-city school.

Finally, the chapter closes with Alyson Sweinhart' story of how the Philadelphia Urban Seminar led her to change her undergraduate major and ultimately become a teacher in inner-city Philadelphia.

I Chose to Stay
Kimberly Smith

"Whataya doin' here you white b-word [Changed by Editor]? What? You think you gonna change me, change us? Nah—you got anotha thing comin'."

On the first day of your career you definitely do not expect colorful expletives to be hurled at you by a child with no more than nine years under his belt, but it is challenges such as these that will make or break you as an inner-city teacher. In my experience, it could break you before you have seen the light of success. You just have to ask yourself—do you have what it takes to come back the next day, and every day after that for the next thirty years?

Having my own classroom was exhilarating, to say the least. As future teachers we spend all of our undergraduate time in someone else's classroom, following someone else's guidelines for teaching, enforcing someone else's rules; thinking all the while that we will be able to duplicate these harmonious classrooms effortlessly when the tables are turned, hoping everything we are learning will come back to us immediately upon stepping foot in our own wonderfully idealistic classrooms.

I walked into my first day of teaching armed with everything that I had learned from my amazing professors in college. Everything that I was sure I would remember flew out the door as quickly as I opened it. I was left alone, teetering at the threshold of my classroom and of my career. That year I learned that what I knew was nothing compared to what I would learn in the next six months. I spent a lot of time hoping my students did not notice the little mistakes I was making here and there. I learned something very valuable that year. It is okay to make mistakes because in between those mistakes are success stories. In the city of Philadelphia we measure our success stories with yardsticks—even though to others they may only be measurable in centimeters.

The Story of G

The aforementioned child with the potty mouth and colorful expletives met me at the door to our classroom before school started on my first day with the above words of encouragement. I never thought I could be so intimidated by a second grader.

Just as I had dreamed, I had completed my student teaching in Philadelphia that fall and graduated from the Indiana University of Pennsylvania a week earlier in December. I made my way through Philadelphia's hiring process and found myself beginning a job on January 2nd, the day after Winter Recess. Throughout that day I was informed that I had been inadvertently assigned to teach a class of emotionally disturbed children—something I knew very little about. I smiled at the principal and told her that I would be fine. I had just graduated a week ago and I needed a job! I also learned from my co-worker next door that I was the 3rd teacher assigned to the class that year. Their first teacher unexpectedly passed away and the long-term substitute I was relieving was pushing 75.

I knew from the beginning that those six months were going to be the most challenging six months of my life. The cards were stacked against me. I was about to embark on the uphill battle of undoing bad habits and undesirable behaviors and replacing them with more favorable ones. To top it off, I was starting in January with a class I did not feel capable of teaching. I thought about telling the principal that I needed to be reassigned. Nevertheless, I chose to stay.

Amongst boys and girls who were growing up in an abusive household, from robbing other people's households, to not having a household to grow up in at all, G was my greatest challenge. He was small in stature, no taller than my shoulder, a very skinny African American boy. He had quite a few missing teeth from a fight that, I later learned, took place in our classroom earlier in the year.

G lived in a single parent home, if you could call it that. His house rarely had electricity and he and his 14-year-old sister shared a deflated air mattress on the floor of their one room efficiency apartment in an area known as "The Badlands" of North Philadelphia. His mom only came by occasionally to drop off food and his dad was upstate serving, what G told me, was a life sentence. Though I never learned what his dad was in for, I gathered that this small child witnessed the crime and that was what earned him a spot in my classroom. It also fueled him with the anger and hostility to make him capable of assaulting anyone who came in his way, including me. Learning all of this about my students and about G's life scared me, I did not know if I could handle the emotional responsibilities that came with teaching this class but again, I chose to stay.

After serving one lunch detention with G after having been hit in the face trying to break up a fight between he and another student, I realized that he, like so many of the other students, was a product of his environment, and that it may be possible to change his behavior. He was actually a sweet kid, who thrived off positive reinforcement. It was as if he had never had anything nice said to him before. That day I began my detention asking him what he had done wrong to have to stay with me at lunch. After discussing the behavior that got him there in detail, I said to him, "G, I expect you to change your behavior from now on and if you cannot do it for yourself, do it for me because I love you." His reaction was one that will be permanently etched in my mind. "You love me? How can you love me? I'm a bad kid, I'm awful and mean, I'm stupid, and I messed up this whole place. I punched you in the face! I'm not worth your time Ms. Smith. You don't have to say that." It became very obvious to me that this blind rhetoric that G was repeating was something that someone had said to him. Someone had almost brainwashed him into thinking that he was a bad seed.

That day I kept G with me during my prep period and we talked and talked. We walked around the school and I learned that G had seen and experienced things that I have only seen in movies and even then I had to cover my eyes. From that day on, we were a team. We made a pact to stay true to each other and to ourselves.

The next few months I tried my best to make the same connection with some of my other students. Often times these fragile boys and girls would let seemingly minor things get under their skin and my classroom would erupt like a WWF wrestling match. I tried desperately to break up these fights but more often than not, I ended up taking a stray punch to the face, or a kick in the stomach. When things like these would happen the administration would file a serious incident report. These reports are made public within the school district for all to see. They clearly do not portray the school in the best way possible. I knew that if this kept happening, there might be a chance that my position would not be secure the following year. But despite the problems I was having with my students, I made it my mission to stop the chaos that was exploding in my classroom daily.

The days turned to months and even the toughest students in my class were learning to get along. We had broken racial boundaries and begun talking and communicating with one another! G tried really hard to change his behavior as well. Other teachers were recognizing him for his outstanding commitment to our pact. Occasionally he got himself caught up in a fight or an argument but this was becoming more infrequent every day. G was making leaps and bounds and his classmates were following in his footsteps!

After trying to quit once a week, shedding endless tears of frustration, and getting bruises from breaking up fights, I finally made to the last week of school! Everyone was settled in their seats when I heard G and another of my students coming back from lunch arguing. It seemed that TK was telling colorful stories about G's older sister. I heard him say, "You know what TK, you ain't worth it. My education is what's worth it and you ain't so I'm out." At that moment I was so proud of G and how far he had come in such a short time. He was repeating everything that I had droned into his brain regularly each day! As they walked down the hallway and entered our classroom I heard TK clear her throat. I looked up and watched her spit right in G's face. With that a huge fight broke out and after waiting fourteen excruciating minutes for an administrator to arrive, as I had been instructed to do, both students were badly injured. TK was sent to the hospital needing stitches in her eyebrow, and G had a black eye and cuts on his neck. As the dean of students escorted him down the hallway, he looked at me directly in the eye and with a split bottom lip he mouthed, "I'm sorry."

I had never been more frustrated in my life. I was frustrated with G and with TK. I was frustrated that I had been instructed not to interfere in any more fights that were going on in our classroom but to wait for administrators. I was frustrated with the administrators for taking fourteen minutes to get there. My frustration grew as the day went on and I can remember feeling like a ball of fire was slowly rising in my body.

I made it through the rest of the day and was never notified of what would happen to G or TK. No one called me to clarify what led up to the incident; there was no request for a pink slip. I suppose the administration had seen their fill of these two particular students and made their decision based on prior incidences. As soon as I dismissed my students to the schoolyard I rushed to the office where I was met by the dean of students, who made it very clear from day one that she felt that I was way over my head. I asked in a panic, "What happened to G? What did you do with him? He never came back for his book bag. Did his mom come to get him?"

She informed me that G had been expelled and would not be returning back to school, and once the principal joined us I was informed that I would not be returning either. It seemed that there were too many "problems" in my classroom and I did not have the classroom management skills to handle it. As much as I could not deny that my class was a challenge and that I sometimes felt ill equipped to handle it, I could not go quietly. I felt that ball of fire rose inside of me and came straight out of my mouth. I could not go down without a fight. I explained that I was not given a fair chance to show my skills and felt that if I had begun teaching in September instead of January my students would have made commendable progress, even though I knew that had made leaps and bounds the second half of the year. I defended my students' progressions and fought for G's right and for my right to stay at that school. I fought for our pact. Unfortunately for me, my words fell on deaf ears.

Completely deflated, I made my way back to my classroom and put my head down at my desk and cried. I cried for G, I cried for the work we had done, I cried that the administration did not care that he had made changes and made big strides throughout the year, I cried for the loss of my job and I cried for every other frustrating thing that happened to me that year. When I was exhausted of crying, I picked up my bag, and left the school.

Upon turning the corner I was surprised to see G. He looked as bad as my beat up 1992 Honda he was standing next to. As I got closer I could see that he was crying, something I had never seen before. I knelt down and gave him a hug and as he sobbed he told me again that he was sorry. He was sorry for letting my down, and for not staying true to our pact. He was sorry he got kicked out of school and he was sorry he would never see me again.

At this point we both cried and after some time I pulled away and looked at him. I wondered why people could not see the innocence in the small child I saw standing before me. Instead, they saw an angry, aggressive and mean kid. I explained to him how proud I was of him and how I would never ever forget him. I told him how much I loved him and how happy he made me. I gave him one final hug and then I stood up and got into my car. His hands slid down my window leaving streaks from the tears he wiped from his face. Through the streaks I took one final look at G, my protégé in the making and I smiled. For G had transformed from a rough around the edges kid to a gentleman; a kind and caring young man who I hoped would always be that way.

I finished the week at that school and never went back. I do however keep in touch with the guidance counselor who remains at that school. G's mom tried to enroll him in third grade the following year and was denied by the administration. He was later taken from his mom and put in foster care. Though I have not seen G since that day, I try to keep tabs on him. Currently, G is in the 4th grade at a Charter School in Philadelphia. I have kept in touch with him over the past few years through letters and phone calls and he is doing quite well. He assures me, and I would like to believe, that it might have something to do with me. To this day I have a picture of G hanging on my refrigerator to remind myself that to this one kid—I made a difference.

After the first six months of my career had ended, I debated about whether I should leave the city and try to take an easier job in the suburbs. Instead, I thought of G and of all of the other students and successes in that tumultuous classroom, and I chose to stay.

I now teach in a school whose magnificence is exemplified by its staff and students. I drive to work each day and look at the people in the cars next to me. No one looks as content as I do because I do not believe that anyone in the cars surrounding me has as fulfilling a job as I do. I am very lucky to have ended up at this school and can feel myself learning, growing and changing every day. I am becoming the educator I always knew I could be.

Teaching is not the kind of profession you choose—it chooses you. If you are lucky enough to be chosen by this rewarding profession, do yourself a favor and stick it out. The first year will be rough; there will be lots of tears, and countless heartache. Think of these as notches on your belt, or tools in your toolbox. It is these experiences that make you a better teacher. Always remember to celebrate your successes, each and every day no matter how small they may seem. You may find yourself wondering, should I stay, or should I go? I chose to stay.

(Kimberly Smith is a teacher at Clara Barton School in Philadelphia.)

Why I Chose to Stay
Shannon Taylor

Even though I feel very comfortable in an urban setting and I was extremely excited to come to the Urban Seminar, my positive feelings quickly changed to frustration, fear, and stress after the long wait, getting lost, confused drivers, lack of information, and even a limited supply of pizza. However, I can note that this first day experience taught me how to remain calm and flexible in high-stress situations, which I feel is an important teacher quality. (Taylor, 2007)

Little did I know at that moment, those words would soon become my everyday reality. The truth is: when teaching in Philadelphia, high-stress situations occur on a daily basis and the ability to stay calm and flexible are crucial. Yet still, I would not change those daily experiences for any other teaching position. I chose to stay.

As a sophomore at Shippensburg University, my teaching experiences in Philadelphia began when I enrolled in the Urban Seminar. Fourteen of us and a professor joined about four hundred other students and their professors at LaSalle University for a two-week urban experience; we lived together in the dorms, we were placed in various classrooms across the district, and we were immersed in the inner-city culture.

The experiences that I faced during those two weeks taught me that teaching is infinitely more rewarding when you have to leap over mountains and rivers to reach a successful ending. I have learned that being able to succeed at and overcome nerve-racking obstacles is the greatest way to experience a feeling of pride and personal fulfillment. In fact, I entered A.K. McClure Elementary School, in the Hunting Park section of Philadelphia, on the first day of Urban Seminar with eager anticipation. That excitement quickly turned into sweaty palms and racing heart beats when I was told that I was assigned to the English-Spanish Bilingual Kindergarten classroom even though I do not speak a word of Spanish. While walking to the classroom, my cooperating teacher Ms. Ruiz explained to me that most of the students were placed in the bilingual setting because they do not speak any English at home. Therefore, the students learned in Spanish on Monday, Wednesday, and Friday, and then in English on Tuesday and Thursday. How was I going to teach these five or six-year-old children in a language that I do not even know how to speak myself? Fortunately, Ms. Ruiz decided to have me primarily work with her highest level group, which was comprised of five students that were fluent in both languages, and I would teach them every day in English only.

Although it was a struggle to communicate through spoken language with every student in the classroom, simply being a smiling face in the classroom everyday was a very easy way to communicate my caring support for each student. In fact, after my seventh day in the school I wrote:

> One of my students that speaks little to no English and is very shy, came up to give me a big hug today. I was shocked! Then for the rest of the day, he continually came up to me to tell me stories in Spanish. Even though I could not fully understand what he was saying, I could tell how excited he was that I was there to listen to him. This reminded me how big of an impact a teacher can actually make in just one student's life.

Overall, yes it was a rather difficult setting in which to teach, but those positive moments with the students make all of the challenges worthwhile.

The eight days that I spent with those five students, as well as the other students in the class, opened my eyes to a whole different world. Not only did the students learn from me, but I also learned from them. Nothing is more rewarding than embracing and accepting a new culture while witnessing the young minds of our future learn from your lessons, experiences, and knowledge. Yes the classroom had metal bars on the window, but the majority of those kindergarten students could read, write, and speak in both English and Spanish. They smiled and laughed as they tried to teach me Spanish, and then they listened and participated as I tried to teach them math, reading, and writing in English. Having the ability to take a glimpse into the traditions and values of other cultures gives me the opportunity to learn something new everyday and ultimately makes me a more well-rounded citizen. Why would I want to teach at the same suburban elementary school that I attended for first through fifth grade when I can open my eyes to another way of life? The thrill of facing a challenge, the feeling of being needed, and the open window into other cultures is what made me decide to stay.

After participating in Urban Seminar, I knew in my heart that I wanted to teach in Philadelphia. I set out to do everything that I could to guarantee myself a job in the City of Brotherly Love. In fact, I took extra credits each semester and applied to West Chester University as a visiting student so that I could student teach in the School District of Philadelphia and graduate from college one semester early. For student teaching I was placed in sixth grade at S.W. Pennypacker Elementary School in the West Oak Lane section of Philadelphia. Most students at this school spoke English, but many also spoke French because they immigrated to America from French-speaking Islands in the Caribbean, such as Haiti and St. Lucia. Another large population of my students was in the foster care system, and unfortunately, the instability of their home life often led to unsteady emotions. Once again, my ability to remain calm and flexible became vital as I faced the obstacles and cultural differences while simultaneously supporting and educating thirty-six sixth grade students.

As my semester of student teaching came to a close, I knew that my time in the School District of Philadelphia had not reached its ending point yet. Therefore, I applied and interviewed with the district. Unlike many of my fellow graduates in December 2008, I knew two days before graduation that I was hired by the School District of Philadelphia.

Currently I am teaching fifth grade inclusion students at J.H. Webster Elementary School, which is in the Kensington section of Philadelphia. My inclusion classroom is unlike any other; I have twenty one students with IEP goals and six other students that are achieving on or slightly below grade level. Among my twenty one learning support students, I have one student with autism, one student with cerebral palsy, three students that are diagnosed mentally retarded, and numerous students with ADD/ADHD, bipolar disorder, and/or emotional disturbances. Reading levels in my classroom range from Kindergarten to fifth grade levels. I am extremely grateful for the courses I took on differentiated instruction in college! During Literacy, some students are working on phonics skills while other students are working collaboratively in Literature Circle groups discussing a chapter book. Then during Math, one group is working on multiplication, another group is practicing addition and subtraction, and the third group is working with money or fractions in word problems. Not only am I making sure that they are learning according to Pennsylvania Standards and their individual IEP goals, but I am also making sure that Tyler does not run out of the school building, and that Josh and Sally had breakfast, and that Quinton does not have a melt down because he was not asked to help, and that Tiffany does not threaten to beat Cindy up after school, and that Jennifer feels safe and wanted as opposed to be afraid and neglected like she is at home.

I am not only a teacher; I am a parent, I am a role model, I am a doctor, I am a counselor, I am a person on whom the students can depend. These students are our future, and if I do not give them the skills to be productive citizens, who will? My students live a very different life than I did as a child, and I learn more about them everyday, but I also open their eyes to the numerous opportunities that the world has to offer them. Every school, whether in an urban, suburban, or rural setting, has its challenges, and the grass is not always greener on the other side. Teaching in the School District of Philadelphia is not for everyone, but the diversity and the challenges of teaching these at-risk students find a special place in my heart. If you love what you do, the passion will pull you through. Yes my job is a challenge, yes I am mentally and physically exhausted at 3:09pm everyday, yes I am under more stress and pressure than I have ever felt before, and yes, I still choose to stay.

(Shannon Taylor is a teacher at J. H. Webster School in Philadelphia.)

Answering the Call: From Philadelphia Student to Philadelphia Teacher
Tysean Gross

I spent most of my life in Philadelphia and being schooled in the School District of Philadelphia. In my neighborhood, it was common for a child to grow up without a father or many other male figures around; it was just how things were. Most of the boys in my neighborhood, including myself, just ran around doing anything we saw fit. Some of us chose to chase after girls, others decided to use or sell drugs, and some of us turned to a life that led from one crime to another. I dealt with most of these activities in some capacity, but for the most part, I decided to stick with school.

I witnessed the downfall of many people around me and knew that I did not want to take the same route that they had. I learned early on that life is what you make of it, and there was something inside of me that yearned for more than what I could see around me. I had passion inside of me. I neither knew what that passion meant, nor was I prepared for the journey it would take me on, but what I did know is that I would never look back once I took the first step toward that journey.

Times were hard growing up, and school had become my safe haven. In school, I had a steady breakfast and lunch, and many friends who shared my same experiences. That alone got me through many years of school, but as I got into high school, life had not gotten any easier and the demand for me to make my way in life had gotten even higher. By that time, in order to make it, I had to make my own money to buy the materials I had needed, and learning algebraic equations and reading stories about people who would never know life from my perspective was not getting the job done. On top of that, school was starting to bore me. The work was never challenging, and I was constantly reminded of the fact that we had significantly less resources than schools in suburban areas. So, I spent less time in school and more time finding my own way. I felt as though obtaining my high school diploma would not do much for my seemingly dead end future, but after a year of trial and error, I decided to stick with it to see where it would take me. Most of my friends were in school with me, and bringing home good grades always made my grandmother proud. So, I figured I would stick with school and make my next move when it was over.

By the time I had officially decided to stick with school, my high school years were half way over. In my junior year of high school, I was very fortunate to have two very skilled teachers who really challenged me. In my life, I have had very few teachers who have affected my life the way they had. One had been my Social Studies teacher, and the other had been my Honors English teacher. Together, they had opened up my world and showed me what great challenges an education could help me to overcome. These teachers define what it really means to be great educators; they really helped to develop me as a student. Aside from being challenged in the classroom, my Social Studies teacher had recommended me for a new program called the *Dwight Evans Civic Leadership Summit*. In this program, we were to come up with a problem within our community, have an action plan for solving that problem, and present it at the Civic Leadership competition. My high school was the only public school in the competition, and our action plan won us the competition. The *Dwight Evans Civic Leadership Summit* opened up many doors for me. Speaking with its representatives as well as my favorite teachers, the possibility of getting into college was dropped into my mind. Through their efforts, I was convinced to take the SAT's. Although I had taken that step, the possibility of going to college was still very faint in my mind. The plan for me to just finish high school and wait to see what happened next was still very much in effect.

My senior year proved to be more difficult than I had anticipated. I had failed to listen to my teachers who advised me to continue to challenge myself and take the new advanced placement (AP) courses my school was offering. I decided through much convincing to take one AP class, AP statistics. My school was also offering AP English as well, but Honors English had been challenging the previous year, and I did not want to take on more than one AP class for fear of failure. I soon regretted that decision heavily. I ended up taking an English class that did not challenge me at all. Till this day, I can not recall one lesson I learned that I was able to carry with me. I had a teacher who was undoubtedly intelligent, but failed to share that knowledge with the students. I hated that class with a passion, and would have done anything to get out of it.

The one memory I will always remember is the day I submitted my senior project. My Social Studies teacher, from the previous year, had given me the idea to do my senior project on the U.S. Patriot Act. It had been passed some time before, but I did not know much about it, so I decided to go for it. I worked really hard on the project, and when I submitted it, my teacher literally thumbed through it and said "Uh, you can do better. I'll give it a B." I was very angry about that, but a B was a passing grade and I had much bigger worries at that time, so I let it go. That experience taught me that hard work only pays off when it is accompanied by persistence. I knew that I should not have allowed that to happen.

At the time, I was still working with the *Dwight Evans Civic Leadership Summit* representatives as well as different school administrators through a Senior Residency program that my school offered to students who had obtained enough credits. While working along side of the representatives and the people within the residency program, I was asked many questions about college. It was February of my senior year and I had not filled out any college applications, had no particular schools in mind, and carried with me the notion that I had no way of paying for college even if I wanted to go. After learning that I had no intensions of furthering my education, they assured me that I was incorrect in my preconceived notions about college, and helped to put me in the right direction. By the time I completed my senior year of high school, I had been accepted into seven different universities. Through a long process, I ended up at Lincoln University, and the rest is history as well as history in the making.

Answering the Call

Becoming a teacher had been in the back of my mind for many years, but I never thought I would actually go for it. School was all I had known, so I passed off my wanting to be a teacher as just an emulation of what I had seen over the years. When I came to Lincoln University, I decided to major in Business Administration. Upon entrance into the university, students are mandated to take a test called the Applegate Test. This test assesses students' reading skills and measures which students would greatly benefit in taking the developmental Reading and Study Skills course. My initial reason for coming to Lincoln University was because the housing situation with the other school I had chosen did not really work out, but I wanted to leave home so badly that I decided to go to Lincoln for a year and then transfer back to the original school I had chosen. Because I had no intensions of staying at Lincoln University for more than a full academic year, I did not care to do well on the Applegate Test. Not taking the test as seriously as I should have got me placed into the Reading and Study Skills class. I was very upset, but within that class I learned much about education. Although the class was not very challenging for me, I enjoyed it and was able to take some lessons away from the class. At the time, I was still a Business Administration major, but I felt so at home in my previous education class that I decided to take Introduction to Education as part of the university's core requirements.

My Introduction to Education class opened up the world of education. I saw myself and my experience within the examples given in class and excelled greatly in the class. While taking Introduction to Education, I seriously considered changing my major from Business Administration to English Education. I felt that with my experiences along with my passion for education, I would be able to make a great contribution to the education world. I was not at all happy with my Business Administration major, and after having a long conversation with my Reading and Study Skills professor, I decided to make the switch. After deciding that I would officially become an education major, I knew I wanted to teach high school students, and my past experiences taught me that many students miss out on the wonders learning English can bring. So, I decided that I would teach English. I had experienced English teachers at their best as well as at their worst. I have dedicated myself to making sure I will be remembered as one of the great ones.

On the Other Side of the Desk: Returning through Urban Seminar

Preparing for a career as a teacher has taken me on a journey I would have never expected. I have learned so many life lessons about myself, my people, and other people as well. I learned not only to tolerate, but embrace those who are different from myself. One of my most memorable experiences on my journey to becoming a teacher was returning to Philadelphia as a student-teacher with the Philadelphia Urban Seminar. I learned much during the Urban Seminar experience, some good and some bad. Walking into my assigned school was unreal. I remember meeting all the staff and looking at the students. I was instantly taken back to my days in high school in the School District of Philadelphia. The school I was assigned to was much like my own Philadelphia high school. It had metal detectors, police officers, and a large population of students fighting the uniform policy. I remember being stopped several times in the hallway for not wearing my school uniform. I was forced to show identification that proved that I was not a student there. One of the memories I will always remember is my first time going into the teacher's lounge. Upon entrance, I was stopped at the door and informed that they did not serve students in that area. I once again had to assure them that I was not a student there. As I entered, I heard a few teachers talking quietly about me. I over heard one of them sarcastically stating, "How is he going to come here and teach when he looks like a student himself?" At that time, I felt more welcomed by the students and the more inexperienced teachers than the veteran teachers. For some reason, I expected the opposite.

On the other hand, the Urban Seminar provided extensive interactions with the high school students. I would walk the hallways on my breaks and ask stray students why they were not in class. They would respond by telling me it was "just the way things were around here." I did not accept that answer, and to my surprise the students responded well to my asking them to return to class. Urban Seminar made me feel like I was already in the profession. I had to prepare and present lesson plans for the students, attend staff meetings, herd stray students off to class, and engage in conversations with other teachers about their feelings toward the school and the students.

One of the most heartbreaking experiences I observed was the fact that some teachers had just given up on the students. I understood greatly the pressures surrounding students growing up in the Philadelphia area. I know how many issues they bring to the classroom everyday they come. I understood them, and they responded well to that understanding. They wanted change as well, but they just did not know where to turn. I could see that in the two weeks I had been there, students were really starting to make positive changes. I did not want the teachers to give up on the students; moreover, I did not want to become like those teachers one day. Till this day, losing my motivation to teach has to be one of my greatest fears. One of my inspirations was my own cooperating teacher. I admire her so much. She was extremely energetic, she had a love for the students, and the students really loved and respected her. She brought so much fun and excitement to her lessons. Although she had only been teaching for a few years, it seemed as though she had been teaching her entire life. She really believed in her students, and that is exactly what they needed. My Urban Seminar experience has showed me what a lifetime of teaching can do. I want to make sure my heart is always in it; that is the only way I will be willing to continue teaching. Although I met a few teachers who have given up the fight, it is teachers such as my cooperating teacher, and other positive teachers I had met at my host school, as well as the dedicated administration that let me know I can really make a difference if I never give up the fight.

Aside from placing me in the classroom, Urban Seminar also placed me around many prospective teachers from other institutions around the state. That was an experience I would not soon forget. I got to know so many people who were different from me. We were able to share and compare our experiences with our journeys to becoming educators. I found that although we came from many different backgrounds, we all had many of the same struggles. They also had experiences like losing friends, broken homes, and having a lack of motivation in school. We also shared the struggle of successfully getting through our teacher education programs. I received ideas about lessons, while sharing advice on how I passed the Praxis exam. I met a variety of prospective teachers during Urban Seminar. Some could not wait to finish their teacher education programs and return to the urban areas to teach, while others felt as though urban teaching was not for them. I discovered one does not have to be from an urban district to understand the struggles students go through: many of our struggles are universal. During the Philadelphia Urban Seminar, I discovered myself as a teacher. My experiences made me more enthusiastic about going into the field. I will carry the lessons I have learned from the Philadelphia Urban Seminar with me forever.

The Final Thought

I believe that everything happens for a reason. If I would not have seen the best and worst of teaching, I more than likely would not have even attempted to become a teacher. All of my experiences growing up in Philadelphia have allowed me to identify with students across all racial backgrounds. I was not always the best student, and I know what it is like to want to quit. I also know what it is like to be great in school and excel. I believe teachers are born. It is a special calling that must and will be answered. I never thought that I would enter myself into a teacher education program, and I certainly never thought it would give me the experiences I have had. I do not know the full extent of my destiny, but I know that as long as I am an educator, I am on the right path.

(Tysean Gross is a student at Lincoln University.)

I Enjoy Teaching in Philadelphia
Stephanie Montalvo

For a long time, being a pediatrician had always been my childhood dream. I wished that one day I would grow up to be a world-renowned pediatrician. Although I did not quite become a pediatrician, I did choose a profession that also involved working with children.

There are no teachers in my immediate or extended family, but when I said I wanted to be a teacher no one was truly shocked either. As a little girl growing up I have fond memories of playing with the girls from the neighborhood. We would play from sunrise to sunset, sometimes even refusing to go in for lunch in fear that we would miss something exciting. Among all our role-playing, my favorite role to play was teacher. We would take all the furniture on the deck and rearrange it so it took on the look of a classroom. We would set up desks and take out all the handouts and workbooks we had salvaged from our own school year. Looking back at it now it makes me laugh to see what tough teachers we portrayed. We would not allow any of our students to talk or even go to the bathroom.

When I look back at my schooling, apart from support of my parents, a few special teachers always come to mind. I had many positive experiences while others did not seem so, but I now realize things happen for a reason and must take the good with the bad. We must learn from all the experiences and people that come in and out our lives. Sometimes as I think about the past, I wonder if the teachers I had over my school career realize how much they had impacted my life and decisions. For example, my Urban Seminar professor, she provided me with an unforgettable experience. She gave me an opportunity to experience children in an urban setting while enrolled in the Urban Seminar. During this seminar we went into Philadelphia's public schools and observed and collaborated with some of Philadelphia's finest. When I first entered the neighborhood of the school I had been assigned to I thought to myself: have I taken a wrong turn? The sidewalks were dirty; there was trash all over the street and many rundown houses. When looking at some of the houses I found myself thinking do people honestly live in these? It was brought to my attention that many of my students came from these very houses. This saddened me, but when I talked to them they did not even think anything of it. They knew nothing else. The place they lived was the same place they had always lived. When I asked the kids to describe the neighborhood to me, the common description included violence that invaded their neighborhood on a daily basis. Many students mentioned not being able to go outside to play for fear of being shot or harassed by junkies and hustlers. I immediately fell in love with the children and could tell they needed me. That moment right there was the reason I chose to stay. I requested the same school to do my student teaching. I began to bring my family into the neighborhood to do community service. We had connected ourselves to the community in hopes to help brighten the futures of many children. Many people will never understand why I teach in the inner city.

As I reflect on my teaching now I feel that I embody all the different characteristics that I learned from others. One must have determination and strive to meet goals, without which it is very hard to be an effective teacher. There have been many times during my teaching career when I sit and think: why is this happening to me? You have to learn from your mistakes and make changes. As a teacher you are a reflective learner, always in a state of self-evaluation. You are constantly embracing constructive criticism from peers, principals and students, and using it in a positive manner to improve your skills. When I was transferred to what is now the school where I work, I was appointed to the K-6 grade science position. I was extremely nervous with the new placement, but I quickly became acclimated. It took a lot of reflecting on how to keep the class under control while doing experiments. This position also proved to be a learning opportunity. I found myself relearning topics with my children. I would spend countless hours at home studying the information the night before so that I would be prepared the next day to present the material to the class. I attended workshops at the Franklin Institute held in the afternoons, on how to teach certain topics out of Foss Kits. I began to enjoy teaching so much that I ended up applying for the Master's Program in Integrated Science Education Program in University of Pennsylvania. Never in a million years did I think I would be going back to school for a science based Master's program, let alone going to University of Pennsylvania. I had always been told that going to University of Pennsylvania was so hard you would never make it, but here I am today. When I reflect on my life I am extremely proud of all my achievements. If it were not for my many events in my walk of life and the people I met along the way, who knows if I would have ever taken this path. I have often wondered "did I choose the path or did the path choose me?"

(Stephanie Montalvo is a teacher at James G. Blaine School, Philadelphia.)

From Urban Seminar to a
Teaching Career in Philadelphia
Alyson Sweinhart

As an undergraduate student at West Chester University, prior to becoming a teacher, I thought that a career in child psychology might be a good fit for me, as I was discovering that I enjoyed being an advocate, helping, and sharing my knowledge with others. After taking a class in Abnormal Psychology, I became interested in studying and working with children along the Autism Spectrum. After a summer job working with children with Autism, I finally figured out that teaching was one way to incorporate all of my aspirations. So, I chose a minor in Special Education, hoping that one day I could make a difference for those children who really needed all of the energy I was willing to put forth on their behalf.

During my course of study in my minor, we had the opportunity to enroll in the Urban Seminar. Confused about this unique experience, I asked around to find out what exactly the program offered and attended two open sessions offered by a faculty member who taught the course. I also wondered how it could assist in my future plans. Once I learned a little more about the Urban Seminar, I immediately signed up for the two-week intensive urban field work in May. However, I have to admit that before it began I was nervous; new faces, a new district that was unlike the one in which I was schooled, and new ideas that I had not learned previously. However, despite the whirlwind of nervousness and excitement, the first Monday morning of the seminar still came. I was placed at a magnet high school in West Philadelphia. As we drove through the neighborhood, I was scared and curious. I saw groups of people, young and old, gathered everywhere. The neighborhood seemed strange to me, different from where I grew up. It was different that a school would be placed right on a main street in the city.

Getting out of the van with the other field students from all over the state, I looked at the building where I would be working for two weeks. It was a beautiful old building, despite bars on the windows. Walking in, I noticed the murals on the walls and the encouraging banners. I met the principal, who was very positive, and learned about the school. Soon, I met with the Special Education Liaison (SEL), a brilliant woman who changed the negative stigma of "learning disabled" in a school where most children did not have to worry about the obstacles of reading or math. She taught me much in the two weeks of Urban Seminar.

Next, it was time to meet the students. As far as first impressions go, students made a pretty good one. They were friendly, well-behaved, and respectful of adults. They made it to class on time; they worked hard and paid attention while in class; they turned in homework. Although this may sound like typical expectations of high school students, I was to work with children with learning disabilities. However, I soon discovered that the students I would be spending two weeks were great! They still had the drive and energy to participate in regular education classes, and only sought help when needed. Their advisor and the SEL encouraged the students to do more each day. It was amazing to see her students light up when they finally understood a challenging topic, and brag when they scored high on a test or paper. This is what I wanted in my life, students that I could brag about too!

By the end of the final days of the Urban Seminar, I learned to get a teaching position "networking" is an important skill. I was so impressed by the speakers of the Philadelphia School District, who addressed the bright-eyed, newly transformed college crowd in the auditorium after our days in the schools, particularly the Administrator of Human Resource, who pumped us up much like a pep-rally. In terms of my recruitment, I was kept in the loop with all of the open houses, hiring events, and mass interviews. I could sense that the School District of Philadelphia was a place that really needed me and everything that I was willing to give.

After graduating from WCU in December, 2008, I had already attended a hiring seminar and had an interview. I was well on my way to making my new dreams come true. In January 2009, I started at a different high school than the one at which I was placed for my Urban Seminar field experience. The morning I began I did not have a classroom yet so I spent my first week in the Special Education office, filing paperwork and doing other tasks. Finally, I was placed into a classroom as the Resource Room teacher, although in my field, I remained somewhat unclear of my expectations and my role in the students' lives. However, under the guidance of my New Teacher Coach, my mentor, I created a new schedule for my students and started an inclusive approach in order to target more of the students. Veteran teachers were initially concerned with this idea, but eventually supported it and saw the benefits.

It had been a crazy, whirlwind six months, but I found an actual purpose for myself. I was helping students in my class. I was making a difference in my students' lives. Today, I am still teaching at this school, and I am helping under credit and over age students get back on track. I am watching the learning light that had once been dimmed gain new energy and vibrancy.

Looking back on my "preparation," I can say that I was not expecting most of what I was confronted with beginning my new teaching position. The Urban Seminar and field experience was an irreplaceable experience for me. I was introduced to new people, new opinions, and new teaching methods. The program encouraged me to pursue a teaching career in an urban area. It allowed me to make connections with important figures in the district, and allowed me the ability to meet some really great students. Although I did not feel that it prepared me completely for my current setting, I am not sure any field can, I learned, however, more about the future district where I wanted to teach. For example, I was able to learn the district's technology and the city's public transportation. Most importantly, I learned how I could relate to the students I might one day teach, and I would remain confident and excited about my teaching career.

Now, these students are "my kids" and I worry about them when they leave at the end of the day. I worry that I will not be able to touch them the way that I was touched by my favorite teachers, but every day, I am encouraged when they show up, ready (and even excited) to learn. The Urban Seminar has given me one of the greatest gifts, the ability to help those children who truly need it, and the ability to help those children who truly appreciate it.

(Alyson Sweinhart is a teacher at University City High School in Philadelphia.)

Chapter Five

Research on Philadelphia Urban Seminar

Chapter Five illustrates research conducted by faculty and students. Without data based analysis it is difficult to assess the effectiveness of the program.

Reporting on the result of quantitative data collected from Philadelphia Urban Seminar participants over nine years, Yong Yu and George Bieger conclude that the Urban Seminar is an effective program for developing pre-service teachers' willingness to teach in our nation's cities. They point out that this carefully designed immersion program, which incorporates cultural knowledge, social participation and school experiences, can significantly change students' concerns and beliefs about urban environments and may serve as a mechanism for increasing the likelihood that students will include inner cities as a teaching career choice.

Employing a very different research paradigm, Michelle Piercy describes her research which examined the content of Philadelphia's murals. Philadelphia has become well known for the murals that decorate many buildings throughout the city. Michelle's concludes that the lives, goals, accomplishments and personal mission of those spotlighted in the city's murals are a memorial not just to a city but to its residents as well. Philadelphia's murals, she notes, are the sum of the city's social issues, history, citizens, role models, politicians, entertainers, athletes, religions, community enterprises and organizations, and ethnicities and cultures.

The Urban Seminar, in addition to being a worthwhile program for preparing new teachers, is also a rich source of data for research on schooling in urban settings. Yong Yu tells how she came to conduct her doctoral dissertation research using the information present in the Urban Seminar. Understanding what makes a good teacher in an inner-city is not an easy task and Yong notes that there is a lot of work to do to be able to understand what makes some urban teachers effective and persistent while others are not so successful at this important task.

In the final article of this chapter, Julie Bao describes how faculty and students from participating universities collaborated in a variety of scholarly and program activities. She points out that, in addition to the research projects and conferences that emerged from this collaboration, perhaps the most beneficial outcome was more personal. She observes that the collaboration, and the bonding among faculty and students that it engendered, underlines the success of the Philadelphia Urban Seminar.

Impact of Philadelphia Urban Seminar on Students' Attitudes and Concerns about Teaching in Urban Schools
Yong Yu and George R. Bieger

Because of growing populations, an aging teaching force, and severe shortages in important subject areas, a growing demand has emerged for teachers in urban settings (Holloway, Rambaud, & Fuller, 1997). This need for teachers prepared and eager to educate urban students is critical, in many, if not most cities across the United States (McCaughtry, Barnard, Martin, Shen, & Kulinna, 2006.). Nevertheless, the task of recruiting qualified teachers who are eager, or even willing, to seek teaching positions in urban environments is becoming increasingly challenging throughout the United States. Many observers attribute this phenomenon to a variety of concerns expressed by pre-service teachers, who might otherwise seek such positions (McCaughtry, Barnard, Martin, Shen, & Kulinna, 2006). These concerns include worries about their personal safety and security, lack of confidence in their ability to cope with the challenges of inner-city schools, concern about the perceived difference in cultural values, and misgivings regarding the ability of schooling to address serious social problems (Waxman, Padron, & Stringfield, 1999).

Although these concerns may be valid and real, they may not be static and instead may be amenable to modification. In their *Stages of Concern* model, Hall and Hord (2001) describe a developmental pattern for how concerns, and the feelings and emotions on which they are based, change over the course of time. According to this model, a person's concerns evolve from being initially focused on "self," then next being focused on the management of a "task," and finally, concerns become focused on "impact," or how the individual can become more effective.

An important key to changing or alleviating students' concerns is understanding the nature and source of those concerns (Oh, Ankers, Llamas, & Tomyoy, 2005). There is considerable evidence to suggest that many student concerns emanate from the misconceptions they have about urban life (Holloway, Rambaud, & Fuller, 1997; Tuggle, 2000) or their reliance on "deficit thinking" (Weiner, 2006). There is no shortage of misconceptions about life in inner cities among the college population, and among the general population overall (Holloway, Rambaud, & Fuller, 1997). These misconceptions, including myths and stereotypes, often prevent pre-service teachers from seriously considering teaching in an urban setting.

The lack of first-hand experiences with different ethnic groups, coupled with socioeconomic problems unique to cities, creates a mindset of fear and intolerance. Thus, if we seek to dispel those myths and stereotypes, it is important to incorporate a variety of avenues for contact between students and inner-city residents (Jorissen, 2003).

The Urban Immersion Experience

The researchers who developed the Philadelphia Urban Seminar believed it was important to increase the contact that participating students would have with the varied and exciting educational practices that often occur within a large city school. By having those students engage, in a comprehensive way, with community, students, teachers, and other school personnel, it was hoped that the immersion experience would develop a group of pre-service teachers who would appreciate and understand the opportunities offered by inner-city schools. The urban immersion experience, from which the data reported in this paper were obtained, includes a set of carefully planned school, community, and cultural experiences. Among the unique features of this program were intensive teaching in inner-city schools, carefully selected professional development activities, and participation in an intensive community service project.

The goals for the Urban Seminar, as described in an earlier paper (Bieger, Vold, Song, & Wang, 2003), were that, as a result of participation in the urban immersion experience, pre-service education students would: 1. Reflect on their previous educational experiences. 2. Collectively identify the educational experience that is characteristic of the dominant culture. 3. Enhance their understanding and appreciation of the complexity of urban culture. 4. Sharpen their qualitative research skills. 5. Identify effective classroom practices by observing and participating in a classroom experience. 6. Become aware of exemplary practices unique to an urban setting. 7. Examine their own value system in a multicultural context, and 8. Participate in a volunteer experience with a cultural group. All these goals helped students reflect on their attitudes and enhance their academic preparations toward teaching and learning in urban environment.

Purpose of the Research

The research reported briefly in the paper examined whether a two-week immersion experience in the inner-city Philadelphia could produce significant changes in pre-service teachers' attitudes, indicated by levels of concerns, toward teaching in urban schools.

Method

In order to determine whether the inner-city immersion experience was significantly effective in changing students' attitudes and alleviating their concerns, a causal comparative study was conducted on an annual basis. The pre- and post-experience questionnaire data reported in this study were collected from pre-service teachers who participated in the Urban Seminar over a nine-year period, and then aggregated and analyzed using multiple statistical procedures which include paired-samples *t-tests, ANOVA* and *correlations.*

Sample. Between 1999 and 2007, 1,262 of the approximately 1,500 undergraduate students who participated in the Philadelphia Urban Seminar completed questionnaires both before participating in the experience and again upon completion of the two-week experience. Figure 5.1 sums up the demographics of the research sample.

Demographics of the sample (n = 1262)					
Gender	Male	Female			
	349	913			
Certification Area	Elementary and Early Childhood	Secondary Education	Dual Certification		No Response
	839	226	109		86
Residence	Urban	Suburban	Small Town	Rural	No Response
	105	490	429	234	4
Taken Multicultural Education Course	Yes	No			No Response
	633	623			6

Figure 5.1 Demographics of the sample

Instrument. A survey questionnaire was the source of data for this study. This questionnaire consisted of 43 items that asked for demographic information and respondents' perceptions, beliefs, and concerns regarding living and teaching in an inner-city setting. Responses were indicated on a five-point modified Likert scale. The questionnaire items were grouped into four categories, assessing participants' concerns about teaching in urban settings on four dimensions: *Concerns about community and cultural differences, Concerns about conditions in the school, Concerns about teaching ability,* and *Personal concerns.*

Procedures. Prior to beginning the urban immersion experience, the students completed the questionnaire. The questionnaire was also given to the students at the end of the experience, thus providing a pre- and post-experience measure of attitudes and concerns. The data were analyzed primarily by comparing pre-experience and post-experience questionnaire responses. Appropriate descriptive data summary and inferential statistical tests were used to conduct these analyses.

Results

Questionnaire responses were analyzed quantitatively to identify possible changes in students' attitudes and perceptions as a result of having participated in the immersion experience. The items from the questionnaire were first grouped into the four clusters mentioned earlier: *Concerns about community and cultural differences, Concerns about conditions in the school, Concerns about teaching ability,* and *Personal concerns.* Then, the data were analyzed to determine whether the program produced any significant differences in students concerns.

Overall change in levels of concern. The first analysis, summarized in the following table, compared the students' pre-experience survey scores with their post-experience scores in each of the four areas of concern. An examination of the means, and the paired-samples *t-test*, indicated significant differences between the pre-experience and post-experience scores in all four of the areas of concern. Student teachers' concern levels were reduced significantly after the Urban Seminar experience. Figure 5.2 illustrates these significant findings.

Comparison of concerns pre- and post-experience							
Category of concerns		Descriptive Statistics			Paired Samples *t-test*		
		Mean	N	Standard Deviation	*t*	df	*p*
Concerns about community and culture	Pre	11.96	1184	3.20	-36.72	1183	<.001
	Post	15.71	1184	4.02			
Concerns about school conditions	Pre	17.01	1198	3.76	-3.165	1197	<.002
	Post	17.45	1198	4.76			
Concerns about teaching ability	Pre	11.27	1209	2.75	-10.78	1208	<.001
	Post	12.36	1209	3.69			
Personal concerns	Pre	18.42	1207	4.44	-21.99	1206	<.001
	Post	21.27	1207	5.22			
Note: A higher number for the mean score represents a lower level of concern.							

Figure 5.2 Comparison of concerns pre- and post-experience

Change in level of concern by gender. Because the sample was obtained from a high proportion of female students, there was a question of whether the finding noted above was true for both male and female participants. Thus, the data were further analyzed on the basis of gender. The results of the analysis of the change of concerns, separately for female and male students, showed convincingly that the concern levels of both female and male students decreased significantly following participation in the Urban Seminar. The one exception was that male students' concerns about school conditions, while they decreased, did not show statistical significance.

Additionally, to determine whether the drop in concern level was different for male and female students, a difference score was calculated for each area of concern, by subtracting the pre-experience score from the post-experience score. These difference scores were then compared. The results of these analyses revealed that the concerns of female students about community and culture, and their personal concerns decreased by a statistically greater amount than male students in both of these categories. There was no significant difference between female and male students in the difference scores for concerns about school conditions or teaching ability.

Change in level of concern for different certification areas. The sample included a higher number of Elementary and Early Childhood Education majors than of secondary majors. Thus, the researchers decided to examine more closely the decrease in concerns, following participation in the Philadelphia Urban Seminar, by examining the scores for each category of major (Elementary/ Early Childhood, Secondary Education, or Dual Certification). The results showed that there were significant differences in all four areas of concern between the pre-experience and post-experience scores for Elementary and Early Childhood Education majors, and in all cases, the level of concern decreased after participation in the experience. The results for students in Secondary Education majors also showed that there was a reduction in students' concerns in all four areas of concern, but that in one category of concern (i.e., Concerns about school conditions); the difference was not statistically significant.

To determine whether the drop in concern level was different for students in the various certification areas, a difference score was calculated for each area of concern, by subtracting the pre-experience score from the post-experience score. These difference scores were then compared among the various certification areas. The results of these analyses revealed that there were no significant differences among the various certification areas regarding the decrease in concerns in any of the four categories of concerns.

Changes in level of concern as a function of residence. The researchers hypothesized that the students' residence, in either a rural, small town, suburban, or urban area might influence their level of concerns. To test this hypothesis, the pre-experience and post-experience scores for students from each type of residence were compared.

The results of these comparison indicated that there were significant differences in all of the concern areas except the area of concern about school conditions. Those student teachers, whose home residence is in an urban area, had less concern about all of the four categories following their participation, though their change in concerns about school conditions did not reach a statistically significant level. Similar results were found about student teachers from suburban areas and rural areas. However, student teachers from small towns showed significant decreases in all areas of concern between the pre-experience and post-experience scores.

In order to determine whether the drop in concern level was different for the various residence areas, a difference score was calculated as described previously. These difference scores were then compared among the various residence areas and the results of these analyses revealed that there were no significant differences among the various residence areas regarding the decrease in concerns in any of the four categories of concerns.

Multicultural coursework. The final area of interest for analysis pertained to whether a student had enrolled in a multicultural education course prior to participating in the Philadelphia Urban Seminar. To test the hypothesis that having taken or not taken a multicultural education course (MEC) might make a difference in concerns, the pre-experience and post-experience scores for students who had taken a MEC and the scores of those students who had not taken a MEC were compared.

The results of these analyses indicated that students who had taken a MEC had displayed significant decrease in all of the four concern areas; while students who had not taken a MEC displayed significant decrease in three of the four concern areas. *Concerns about School Conditions* was the area where the students who had not taken a MEC showed no significant decrease. Nevertheless, when the decrease scores of both groups were compared, there was no significant difference between students who had taken a MEC and those who had not taken a MEC.

The results presented here show that in almost every analysis, and in every category of concern measured, there was a significant decrease in the expressed level of concern. Moreover, the results show that this effect was widespread, and not limited by gender, certification area, residential type, or whether a student had prior coursework in multicultural education.

Conclusions

The most evident and striking conclusion to emerge from the analyses of the survey data from this program is that the Philadelphia Urban Seminar has clearly demonstrated its effectiveness in alleviating many of the concerns that students have about living, working, and teaching in urban settings. An immersion experience, even one of such short duration as two weeks, can have a noticeable and substantial impact on students' concerns and attitudes toward teaching in inner-cities.

In each of the four areas of concern: *Concerns about community and cultural differences, Concerns about conditions in the school, Concerns about teaching ability,* and *Personal concerns,* the data clearly showed decreases in the levels of those concerns following participation in the Urban Seminar experience. The multi-faceted character of the program is, as some researchers suggest, a likely key feature that has contributed to the effectiveness of this program (Tabachnick & Zeichner, 1993).

These findings are consistent with and support the *Stages of Concern* model proposed by Hall and Hord (2001), which suggested that people's concerns evolve as their involvement increases.

In an article entitled "Getting to we: Developing a transformative *urban teaching* practice", Kelly Donnell argues that learning to teach in an *urban* setting is a complex process that is enhanced when beginning teachers develop a transformative *teaching* practice which emphasizes "we." This idea recognizes that in a genuine learning community, learning is mutual, between teacher and pupils (Donnell, 2007). This mutuality is central to the Philadelphia Urban Seminar and is a key underpinning of the program's several components. The careful combination of planned school, community, and cultural experiences that characterize the Philadelphia Urban Seminar has been shown, in the analyses presented here, to have successfully modified the perceptions of students toward teaching in urban settings.

The Philadelphia Urban Seminar has clearly demonstrated its effectiveness in helping develop pre-service teachers' willingness and readiness to teach in our nation's cities. These new teachers, it is hoped, will help create and maintain urban school cultures where "courageous commitment to excellence is fostered and nurtured" (Duncan-Andrade, 2004, p. 349).

Based on the results of this study, it can be confidently concluded that a carefully designed immersion program, which incorporates cultural competence, social participation as well as school experiences, can significantly change students' concerns and beliefs about urban environments and may serve as a mechanism for increasing the likelihood that students will include inner cities as a teaching career choice.

References

Bieger, G.R., Vold, L.A., Song, W. & Wang, D. (2003). Changes in student attitudes and concerns toward inner-city teaching as a result of participation in an urban immersion experience. In Hall, N. & Springate, D. (Eds.) *Proceedings of the 13th Annual Conference of the European Teacher Education Network*, London: Greenwich University Press.

Donnell, K. (2007). Getting to us: Developing a transformative *urban teaching* practice. *Urban Education, 42*(3), 223-249.

Duncan-Andrade, J. (2004). Toward teacher development for the urban in urban teaching. *Teaching Education, 15*(4), 339-350.

Hall, G.E., & Hord, S.M. (2001). *Implementing change: Patterns, principles, and potholes.* Boston: Allyn and Bacon.

Holloway, S., Rambaud, M.F., & Fuller, B. (1997). *Through my own eyes: Single mothers and the cultures of poverty.* Cambridge, MA: Harvard University Press.

Jorissen, K.T. (2003). Successful career transitions: Lessons from urban alternate route teachers who stayed. *The High School Journal, 86*(3), 41-51.

McCaughtry, N., Barnard, S., Martin, J., Shen, B., & Kulinna, P. H. (2006). Teachers' perspectives on the challenges of t*eaching* physical education in u*rban* schools: The student emotional filter. *Research Quarterly for Exercise & Sport, 77* (4), 486-497.

Oh, D. M., Ankers, A. M., Llamas, J. M., & Tomyoy, C. (2005). Impact of pre-service student teaching experience on urban school teachers. *Journal of Instructional Psychology 31*(1), 82-98.

Tabachnick, B. R., & Zeichner, K. M. (1993). Preparing teachers for cultural diversity. *Journal of Education for Teaching, 19*(2), 113-125.

Tuggle, M.B. (2000). *It is well with my soul: Churches and institutions collaborating for public health.* Washington, DC: American Public Health Association.

Waxman, H.C., Padron, Y.N., & Stringfield, S. (1999). Teaching and change in urban contexts. *Teaching and Change, 7*(1), 3-16.

Weiner, L. (2006). Challenging deficit thinking. *Educational Leadership, 64*(1), 42-45.

(Yong Yu is a doctoral candidate at Indiana University of Pennsylvania; George R. Bieger is a professor at Indiana University of Pennsylvania.)

Mural Research in Philadelphia
Michelle Piercy

Home sick for tranquility and for South Central PA's wide open green spaces, and long, uninterrupted stretches of rolling highways and back roads, I phoned my husband at the end of the fifth day of the Philadelphia Urban Seminar seeking the comfort of his familiar voice. Balancing my cell phone to my ear while leaning back on a plastic dorm chair with my feet propped up on the sill of the large hallway window, I noticed a magnificent mural a few blocks away from La Salle University. It featured soaring monarch butterflies against a clear blue sky. "How beautiful," I silently thought. Initially I believed the painting to be an advertisement but later learned that it was one of Philadelphia's famed and prolific murals. As I travelled throughout the city over the course of the next week, I noticed several more murals, no two alike and each a piece of the city's mosaic. I would later learn that the murals represented the social issues, history, citizens, role models, politicians, entertainers, athletes, religions, community enterprises and organizations, and ethnicities and cultures that *are* Philadelphia.

Participation in the 2007 Philadelphia Urban Seminar helped me to recognize the limited scope of exposure to diverse urban cultures that residing most of my life in suburban and rural areas did not afford. Consequently, I felt it important to gain a more in-depth understanding of African- and Latino-American cultures in order to enhance my teaching effectiveness among students whose ethnic and cultural experience differs from that of my own. Many of Philadelphia's murals, I realized, were an ideal instructional tool as they reflected the values, inspirations, issues and role models important to African- and Latino-Americans living in the city. A research opportunity seven months later would bring me back to Philadelphia to take a closer look at the city's magnificent murals and the messages they convey.

My research proposal, entitled *Research on Inspirations and Role Models in Philadelphia Murals,* had as its purpose "to find African-/Latino-American role models in Philadelphia murals and learn about their inspirations and reflected social issues so as to enhance understanding of student teachers, establish better bonding between student teachers and culturally diverse students, and increase teaching accountability in elementary classrooms." A power point presentation I gave at the Urban Education Conference sponsored by the PA State System of Higher Education in March 2008 in Harrisburg, and a poster display of my research at the Shippensburg University Student Research Program Recognition Day in April 2008 culminated my research project. The latter two presentation opportunities were gratifying, but returning to Philadelphia and exploring its murals was really the most rewarding dimension of the research project.

On a seasonably cold but pristinely clear December day in 2007, I returned to Philadelphia where photos were taken and notes recorded revealing recurring themes, messages, and role models in the murals depicting African- and Latino-American cultures in the city. One such mural, located on the exterior of William McKinley Public School, was discovered after a wrong turn down a one-way alley. The mural consisted of the alphabet, solar system, and animals, plus a collage of children's faces of many ethnicities. The alphabet and animal murals included Spanish and English language labels. And the collage of children encircled a quote by Marian Wright Edelman which read, "Education is for improving the lives of others and for leaving your community and world better than you found it." Of that particular community, I have concluded from the messages of its school's murals that the diversity of the many cultural and ethnic backgrounds of its students is valued. Furthermore, it is apparent that the community understands education's positive influence on the individual, on the community, and on the world at large.

Messages of Philadelphians' heritage abound on house and building exteriors throughout the city. Murals covered two- and three-story buildings that spanned the length of entire city blocks. One mural, entitled *Latinoamerica—Una Lengua, Multiples Cultures* (Latin America—One Language, Many Cultures), painted against a light blue background, contained portraits of and quotations by well-known Latino military and political figures, authors, and a textile artist. It featured a bold, vibrant map of the Caribbean, and Central and South America with each Latino country painted in different pastel colors. Important cultural and industrial aspects of individual Latino nations, like various forms of dance, Aztec statuary, and hand-made textiles, were featured in the murals.

All of the mural's quotations were written in Spanish. Simon Bolivar, famous for liberating from Spanish monarchy the pre-South American colonies known in the 1800s as Spanish America, is one prominent Latino quoted on the mural. The quote attributed to Bolivar and included on the mural reads, "Una persona sin estudios es un ser incompleto." Translated into English, the words of Bolivar warn that the person without studies, or an education, is an incomplete being. As a pre-service teacher, this quote especially resonates with me since I too believe that education is vital to each person's complete development. That Latin America's most well-known, historical military and political figure said what he did of education lends significant credibility to its value in the lives of Bolivar's fellow Latinos living in Philadelphia.

Additional depictions of Latino culture represented by various national flags, native dress, landscape, music and dance, holiday celebrations, and foods are found on murals throughout Philadelphia. Such united but individualized representations of Philadelphia's several Latino cultures delineates differences among the various nationalities comprising the city's Latino American population. Although most of the city's public schools follow a school uniform policy, murals' messages of individuality and distinct identity abound for Latino children and can be found in the very neighborhoods where they live and attend school.

African-Americans are also well represented in Philadelphia's murals. Murals portraying African Americans include well-known authors, musicians, athletes, actors, comedians, and political and social leaders whose lives and works are represented in the art. Beyond their literary, musical or athletic accomplishments, many of the individuals featured were significant contributors to the Civil Rights Movement in this country. As well, several African-American athletes and entertainers featured in some murals were pioneers in their sport or art and have become revered role models for peoples of color.

Temple University's poet-in-residence, Sonia Sanchez is a prolific African-American author, poet, speaker, educator, and advocate of issues important to black Americans and is featured in the mural *Sonia Sanchez Family & Friends*. Sanchez is highly educated and acclaimed for her work with, among other organizations, the Black Arts Movement and the Civil Rights Movement as well as issues related to women's rights. Other significant images included with the portraits of Sanchez in the mural are a member of the Black Panthers flanked by two American flags, Bill Cosby, and the profile of Tupac encased in a human heart. The phrase, "resist, resist, resist" appears twice as well as one of Sanchez's haikus dedicated to two of her children, Mungu and Morani, and "the children of Soweto." The haiku reads:

may yo seasons be
long with endless green streets and
permanent summer legs.

In this poem, I hear a mother's hope for the longevity and vitality of her children. Globally, I also glimpse Sanchez's concern for "the children of soweto," youth whose clash with South African authorities in Soweto in June 1976 over unfair education policies resulted in many fatalities and injuries there. Finally, I imagine the haiku is meant also for the children of Philadelphia that their lives be long and fruitful, filled with goodness and bounty.

It would take months to properly study all of Philadelphia's 3,000 plus murals. Of the dozen or so that I studied during my research trip, I discovered layers of significant messages about the African- and Latino-American cultures that make up a large portion of Philadelphia's population. The murals are truly educational tools and reflect what has most shaped and influenced the lives of Philadelphia's African- and Latino-Americans.

By observing and studying which African- and Latino-American role models were highlighted, I gained understanding of each culture's pride in those individuals and what they represent. The lives, goals, accomplishments and personal mission of those spotlighted are a memorial to not just a city but to its residents also. Truly, Philadelphia murals *is* the sum of its social issues, history, citizens, role models, politicians, entertainers, athletes, religions, community enterprises and organizations, and ethnicities and cultures. Consequently, taking the time to look closer at the inspirations, role models, and messages found in the city's murals will give the observer an education in cultures different from his or her own.

(Michelle Piercy is a student at Shippensburg University.)

My Dissertation on the Philadelphia Urban Seminar
Yong Yu

"I went to Philadelphia as a naïve girl from rural country with a mission to help the children and to teach them what I know. I came out having been taught by them and having been helped by them."

"I cannot wait to come back and spend more time here in the schools working with these kids and making a difference, no matter how small it is. I don't want to be in a job where the kids are going to succeed with or without me."

– Philadelphia Urban Seminar participants

When I saw the above comments, I had just started my doctoral studies in Curriculum and Instruction at Indiana University of Pennsylvania and was working as a Graduate Assistant. Based on my previous teaching and research experience, I believed that a program that received controversial or powerful feedback was very likely to be one worth further examination. That was why I was attracted to the Philadelphia Urban Seminar three years ago.

Although I was open to any topic that might come up while assisting in planning, implementing, and evaluating the Urban Seminar, I was also expecting to find an issue that was interesting and significant enough to be a potential dissertation topic. I did not find ONE – I found more than one. There were so many different issues going on during the two-week experience that any of them could be developed into a dissertation study. Why did some teacher-education students believe they could teach effectively in urban schools while others did not? Why were some participants willing to take the challenges of living outside their comfort zones while others complained all the time? What caused some individuals to decide they would like to teach in an urban setting, but turned others away from urban schools when both groups participated in the same activities? Why some participants collected very positive gains from the Urban Seminar, while others walked away with their negative perceptions of urban schools and urban students reinforced?

My initial assumption was that it was different individual characteristics that contributed to the different choices in terms of where to teach. Moreover, the specific choice of teaching in a specific school setting might not be necessarily related to the effectiveness of a teacher so long as the choice matched his or her particular characteristics. For example, some individuals were willing to teach in urban schools and they could become dedicated and effective urban teachers; some other individuals, however, would like to teach in non-urban schools but they could also be very effective and committed teachers in their chosen education settings. It was undoubtedly true that many teachers had left urban schools due to job dissatisfaction resulting from poor school conditions. Nonetheless, it might also be true that their leaving was caused by the mismatch between their individual characteristics and their choice of schools. Teachers who were not willing to teach in urban schools would take the earliest opportunity to leave after they chose to, or were assigned to teach there.

I was very excited at the idea. The possibility of finding those characteristics would be significant in a number of ways. It would benefit the administrators in teacher education programs, school districts, and schools in selecting the right candidates for teacher education studies and/or to teach in schools of particular geographical locations. Individuals could also benefit from the study since it could help them better understand their needs in terms of career choice. Most importantly, if the desirable characteristics, for instance, characteristics positively related to teaching in urban schools, could be changed through certain educational activities such as field experiences in diverse settings, teacher education programs would be able to include those activities and, therefore, would be able to prepare teachers for all settings effectively.

Excited as I was, the design of the study remained challenging. The potential sample for the study, the participants of Philadelphia Urban Seminar, were students enrolled in teacher-education programs rather than in-service teachers. What data could serve the purpose of my study and what instrument should I use to collect the data? My first plan was to develop an instrument by interviewing certain number of effective teachers who were teaching in urban and non-urban settings, including those who started teaching in urban schools but transferred to and stayed in non-urban schools. The teachers could be identified with the recommendation of their principals and colleagues. Based on the interview data, the characteristics of effective teachers in urban and non-urban schools would be described and included in a survey instrument that would be used to measure the Urban Seminar participants' intention to teach or not to teach in urban settings.

This early plan, however, was never implemented due to its limitation and lack of feasibility. It was limited in the sense that the teachers on whom such an instrument might be based would identify characteristics that may no longer be applicable to the current generation of teachers. Therefore, the instrument might not be a valid tool to serve the purpose of the study. Besides, the plan seemed a bit ambitious. It would involve two or three samples, each of which had very distinctive demographic characteristics. Instead of two parts of one dissertation study, the section of instrument development and data collection could be two individual studies.

While I was frustrated by the unavailability of an appropriate instrument to use for data collection, I came across a study conducted by two Australian researchers (Watt & Richard, 2007) to validate a scale measuring motivation factors contributing to the choice of a teaching career. The scale, Factors Influencing Teaching Choice (FIT-Choice) scale, was developed on the basis of expectancy-value model, a motivational framework initially constructed by Eccles and colleagues (1983) to explain achievement motivation. They suggested that an individual's academic choice was mainly motivated by expectation for success and the task valuation. Watt and Richardson extended the original expectancy-value model to the field career choice of pre-service teachers. The FIT-Choice scale consisted of 60 items, organized under four different constructs. In a series of studies in which the scale was applied, Watt and Richardson found individuals' success expectancies and the social and personal values they held about teaching were not only related to their choice of being a teacher, but also their engagement, commitment, and persistence in the profession (Richardson & Watt, 2006; Watt & Richard, 2007, 2008). Based on their findings, I hypothesized that an individual teacher's expectation and values also contributed to his or her choice to teach or not to teach in a particular education setting and the FIT-Choice was, therefore, could be used to collect data for my study.

As the instrument relies on self-reports, as many survey instruments did, I was concerned that participants would not indicate openly that they chose to teach because of job security and long summer vacation. To ensure that the data could serve the purpose of the study to the maximum extent, I decided to include a follow-up interview among the Urban Seminar participants who responded to the survey. I was hoping that some qualitative data could offer some in-depth information about the participants.

All data needed for the study have been collected so far, with the support of numerous people. My advisor and other committee members have always been with me throughout the process of the study, offering help ranging from valuable advice for research design to emotional support. The coordinators from more than 18 participating universities all over Pennsylvanian have been very positive about the study and provided critical support for data collection. Among approximately 500 students that participated in the Philadelphia Urban Seminar in the summer of 2009, nearly 60 percent took both the pre- and post- surveys. More than 200 participants volunteered to participate in the follow-up interview, among which 11 were interviewed.

The analysis of the survey and interview data is still in progress at this point. Although it is too early to draw a conclusion, a preliminary analysis of the qualitative data indicates that factors such as love for children and a strong desire to make difference are common motivational factors that influence the participants' choice to become teachers. Several participants came to the Urban Seminar to test whether teaching in an urban setting is right for them. Hannah, a girl who grew up in a rural area, told me that she was drawn to urban education by the passion and needs that students have in their eyes to learn, "a look in a child's eyes that I have never seen in any other settings." She commented that oftentimes urban children are overlooked because many people do not want to teach in urban settings. As a result, some teachers teaching there are inexperienced and who do not really want to be there, and "that is hurting the children." She believed that each of these children has great potential and there need to be excellent teachers to encourage them, "to make them feel that they are here for a reason; they can make difference in the community; and they can make difference in their own lives."

There is clear evidence about changes before and after the pre-service teachers' participation of the Urban Seminar experience. Some participants came with fear for city life and urban students and suspect whether they would be able to survive the urban classrooms. As they experienced more in the schools and the city, they began to change. At the end of the first week, Alana told me, "these kids are truly not what people think and not what you would imagine when you hear 'urban students.' They will listen, they will treat you with respect, they are incredibly bright and intelligent, they want to learn, they care about their education and their futures, and other than the few, standard expected behavior problems that are found in all young teenagers, they are very well behaved. I found out that it is not what people think, and Philadelphia is not as bad as I thought it would be." Many other participants were like Alana—coming to urban setting with the desire of making difference, only to find urban children have made difference in their life. As Alana said, "I am beginning to definitely rethink my decision to teach in a rural area because I have found that the kids are amazing and anywhere that I am needed the most is where I want to be."

It is worth noticing that not every experience is pleasant. However, I am very pleased to see many pre-service teachers handled these experiences in a positive way. Katelyn, a junior who has been living all her life in a small town, went to school on the last day and was informed a student in the school committed suicide the night before. She recalled, "I feel impenetrable and unrelenting feelings of helplessness as I realize how true the words of Salome Thomas-El ring out, 'Nothing can prepare you for the

day that you see the empty seat where a child will never sit again.'"
But the incident strengthened rather than weakened her motivation
to teach. Katelyn said to me firmly, "If there were ever any doubt
in my mind that the sole purpose of my life is to educate and serve
the future leaders of our nation, after this experience, it has been
entirely eradicated. I have realized my place is here. This is where
they need teachers who are unafraid of change and unafraid of
putting in as much time as possible."

There is a lot of work for me to do to be able to understand
how these pre-service teachers grow through the two-week
Philadelphia Urban Seminar, particularly, why and how positive
changes happened to some but not others. Fortunately, many
participants like Katelyn left me with immense encouragement
to pursue my dissertation study and my career as a teacher
educator. Her final comments truly reflect the impact of a
powerful urban field experience on a teacher's growth:

> I can sincerely say that a grade will never be able to
> show how much I learned and how my life will forever
> be affected by the people that I met during my time in
> Philadelphia. I have grown and matured an immeasurable
> amount as both a teacher and an individual. I have become
> so much more culturally involved and have eradicated all
> of my negative misconceptions about urban areas. I walk
> away from this experience so proud of the progress that I
> have made and ready to, as the famous quote by Mahatma
> Gandhi says, "Be the change that I wish to see in the
> world."

References

Eccles, J., Adler, T. F., Futterman, R., Goff, S.B., Kaczala, C. M.,
    Meece, J., & Midgley, C. (1983). Expectancies, Values and
    academic behaviors. In J.T. Spence (Ed.), *Achievement and
    Achievement Motives* (pp.75-146). San Francisco, CA: W.H.
    Freeman & Company.

Richardson, P.W., & Watt, H. M. G. (2006). Who choose teaching and why? Profiling characteristics and motivations across three Australian universities. *Asian-Pacific Journal of Teacher Education, 34*(1), 27-56.

Watt, H., & Richardson, P. (2007). Motivational factors influencing teaching as a career choice: Development and validation of the FIT-Choice Scale. *Journal of Experimental Education, 75*(3), 167-202.

Watt, H. M. G., & Richardson, P.W. (2008). Motivations, perceptions, and aspirations concerning teaching as a career for different types of beginning teachers. *Learning and Instruction, 18*(5), 408-428.

(Yong Yu is a doctoral candidate at Indiana University of Pennsylvania.)

Faculty Collaborations on Urban Education Conferences and Books
Julie Q. Bao

One of the salient characteristics of the Urban Seminar is its multi-faceted collaborations among participants. With hundreds of pre-service teachers, dozens of faculty members, scores of cooperating teachers from over 60 Philadelphia schools and numerous community facilitators passionately involved in the Urban Seminar every year, collaborations were abundant. Among academic collaborations were faculty team teaching, joint school supervision, annual pre- and post-surveys, a nine-year longitudinal study, several doctoral dissertations, large and mini urban education conferences, and two books. This article focuses on the PA Urban Education Conference and two books on the Urban Seminar accomplished jointly by participants via faculty collaborations.

Collaboration on the Urban Education Conference

The Urban Education Conference of 2008 was initiated during the second week of the 2007 Urban Seminar at Philadelphia. By then, the Seminar had attracted about 500 pre-service teachers and 30 faculty members from 21 universities. With 15 years of accumulated exciting activities and soul searching reflections, participants wanted eagerly to have a venue to share their profound learning experiences. Meanwhile, the tremendous impact of the Urban Seminar needed to be communicated to more stake holders of urban education. To this end, some faculty coordinators proposed a state-wide Urban Education Conference. At the initial stage of the preparation there were some concerns among professors regarding the conference planning, time coordination, and most of all, the much needed state funding. After some preliminary discussions on the necessity and feasibility among coordinators, faculty unanimously supported the conference proposal. Other than believing the merits of the conference, the faculty's support at the time was largely based on the conviction that we have a unique program and an extraordinarily passionate group of faculty coordinators, whose remarkable collaboration would make the conference possible with or without the state funding. True enough, the subsequent planning, budgeting and execution of the conference demonstrated the astonishing power of faculty collaboration and impact of the program.

Conference planning. One of the difficult tasks for preparing a conference is that the organizers are not sure how many people will show up on the day of the conference, and how many presenters will quit at the last minute. They usually rely on association membership loyalty and prepaid registration fees to encourage conference attendance. But we could not collect membership dues, nor could we charge conference registration fees from our students. Yet, this seemingly sizable dilemma was dissolved quickly when faculty pooled collaborative efforts. In fact, the collaboration of faculty coordinators turned out to be such an asset that has not only made the Urban Education Conference possible, but it also made its preparation and execution process more efficient. Jointly planning the conference date is one of the examples.

Planning a conference usually starts with a conference date, which is the first hurdle for conference organizers to clear as the dates will so often run into each other's multiple commitments. In this case, however, it becomes an advantage. With coordinators from 20 universities all represented at the faculty meetings in Philadelphia, we were able to decide on the spot that we would hold the conference in spring of 2008, instead of fall of 2007, to give all universities more time to advocate the conference and write proposals. After the conference's season was chosen, a professor went to a nearby Wal-Mart and picked up a huge monthly calendar. She asked all faculty members present to cross out their inconvenient dates for the spring of 2008. When the cross-out game was over, there were literally only two days left on the calendar: March 18 and 19. Hence these were the two days for the conference. Consequently, all coordinating professors present and the universities they represent were able to attend. Through these faculty members, at least one van of students would be able to attend, which guaranteed a decent base number of participants for the conference.

Selecting subthemes for the conference was another collaborative effort. Preliminary subthemes were proposed at a joint faculty meeting at Philadelphia. Large self sticking sheets were spread on the desks and posted on the walls of the meeting room. All faculty members were free to list and combine their favorite themes and topics in a hands-on method. Through a few rounds of revision at faculty meetings, later via emails, all faculty coordinators agreed to the basic five subthemes for the conference, which included Managing Urban Classrooms, Overall Urban Seminar Research, Teaching and Learning in Urban Classrooms, District/University/Community Partnerships and Working with

Culturally/Linguistically Diverse Children plus a New Urban Teacher Panel.

After conference themes were announced, all faculty coordinators served on the Conference Proposal Screening Committee. Each professor communicated with Urban Seminar participants in their university, encouraged them to share their reflections and previewed students' proposals. When the preliminary screening was over professors of each university submitted student proposals to the Conference Proposal Committee and jointly made the proposal acceptance decisions.

While teamwork effectiveness was evident in the proposal screening and acceptance procedures, the conference registration process benefited even more from faculty collaboration. To total the number of pre-service teachers who would participate in the conference, the Registration Facilitator only needed to send a spreadsheet template to all faculty coordinators on other campuses. Those professors, who knew their students best, collected data and filled out the detailed information of their students on the template. Upon returning of the data, the Registration Facilitator only needed to aggregate the data via a quick cut-and-paste on a master spreadsheet to complete an accurate final list of faculty and student attendants for the conference. The efficiency and accuracy of the registration process was remarkable. Of course we also had to compile a list of conference attendants from outside Urban Seminar participants, which included administrators and cooperating teachers in Philadelphia schools, university deans and department chairs, professors from PA State System of Higher Education (PASSHE) as well as some participants from other states. For that part of coordination, we gladly gave it to the PASSHE Office, which sent them a more formal invitation with her impressive PASSHE seal.

Conference budget. By the time faculty coordinators had decided to hold the conference all 2007-2008 PASSHE's available grants had been allocated, in another word, no more grants for which we could apply in that academic year. Nevertheless, by that time, faculty had already been amazed by what collaboration had enabled us to accomplish, so we were not going to back down on the conference initiative. We were confident that with our collective wisdom, passion and efforts, we could hold the conference with or without extra state funding. So the conference planning went on with a zero dollar budget scenario.

To work with a zero dollar budget, the Conference Committee had to find a free conference venue, preferably centrally located in Pennsylvania. In the process of looking for free conference sites, a professor found out that there were six meeting rooms in the PASSHE's headquarters in Harrisburg, also known as the Dixon Center, which could be borrowed by faculty with a good cause. The Urban Education Conference definitely qualified for a good cause, so without any hesitation, the Conference Committee reserved all six meeting rooms the next day. We were very lucky in securing these rooms, because classrooms were generally booked a semester before, the fact that our conference dates set eight months before gave us the edge to reserve these rooms a step ahead of other classes or training workshops.

With the conference dates and basic rooms secured, the Conference Committee knew the conference was feasible. Furthermore, we knew there was a hidden rule in the PASSHE system that if there is a state wide conference with a good cause, if most universities would go, the home university would be pressured to sponsor. In this case, there was a passionate lobby force on each campus, and many professors and students were eager to attend the conference. Consequently, if each university could send one van, and each college dean could pay for the gas and lunch cost, which was well within the discretionary funds of college deans, there would be a sizable conference. Additionally, there are six private universities among the Urban Seminar groups, which would also send students and faculty to the conference. For participating administrators, paying their own one-day conference within PA is never a big issue. At this stage, faculty coordinators could almost see the conference. We were just amazed by the power of our collaboration.

Nevertheless, the Conference Committee would love to have the State support to increase the scale and impact of the conference. Hence, a professor wrote a proposal to PASSHE. Since all PASSHE grants for the academic year had been distributed; she had no place to which she could send her grant application. Instead of quitting, she checked the PASSHE website and took it directly to the PASSHE Chancellor's Office. She lobbied PASSHE's Associate Vice Chancellor in charge of teaching and learning, who was also the Director of University and School Programs. She pointed out that it was for PASSHE's interest to support a cause so vital. She added that letting faculty of all PASSHE universities organize such a grand conference on their own without showing any state support would make PASSHE look completely out of this political world. When asked how much the Conference Committee was requesting, she presented a menu of four budget options: 1.Zero dollar from PASSHE: A one-day conference held in the six reserved seminar rooms at the PASSHE headquarters in Harrisburg, and each college dean of education would send a van of students and pay for their gas and lunch. 2. PASSHE would pay for the conference lunch, which shows a minimum gesture of support from PASSHE. 3. PASSHE pays for a two-day conference meals and meeting rooms in a hotel, which would expand the conference scope and increase program impact, and 4. A two-day conference plus distributing our first urban education book at the conference.

The Associate Vice Chancellor of PASSHE at the time happened to be an enthusiastic supporter of Urban Education. He listened patiently to the lobbying argument of the professor, a faculty member he had never seen or heard before, and turned around within two days with the biggest support possible for the conference. With the strong support from PASSHE, we moved from a one-day conference at six scattered seminar rooms of Dixon

Center to a grand two-day conference in Holliday Inn East in Harrisburg with all cost covered.

Conference execution. On the day of the Conference, the execution of the plan was a complete pleasure with collaboration of all faculty and students. The Edinboro faculty member led a group of ten students who were also in charge of the Registration Table. They padded the registration folders with all kinds of decorations, and flanked the tables with glaring posters. Despite their eight hours of driving to the conference, they were the first group to arrive and last one to leave.

Presentation equipment usually is a big ticket item for all conferences. But for this one, it is not an issue at all. All universities have basic computers and projection equipment. To coordinate equipment, the Conference Committee developed a list, on which each faculty member signed up earlier to indicate who would bring what equipment, which provided all breakout rooms with adequate equipment plus three sets of spare ones. In addition, all faculty coordinators served as Chairs for presentation sessions. What was unique for this conference was that faculty also signed up for Office Hours on a one-hour rotation base to sit in a large seminar room in the hotel to take care of all travel gears of students, presentation equipment, questions from attendants, or any issues on hand.

As a result, faculty members were not only conference participants; they felt they jointly owned the conference. Apart from keynote speeches and 47 concurrent presentations, each faculty member also sponsored a university booth where their students illustrated exciting learning impact materials and explained them passionately to other participating teachers, students and administrators. These booths and decorations made the conference more like a learning festival than a regular conference. Needless to say, the conference was a huge success. Until now, faculty coordinators and students are still enthusiastically talking about the learning excitement demonstrated at the conference.

Figure 5.3 Urban Seminar students at the Conference

Faculty Collaboration for Urban Education Books

Preparing Urban Teachers Collaboratively in Philadelphia is the title of the first book compiled jointly by Urban Seminar participants. As its subtitle suggests, it is about Urban Seminar related practice, research and reflections. It introduces the development of the Urban Seminar, describes its impact on participants, reports multiple studies, depicts university, school and community partnerships, and highlights a variety of learning experiences of students.

Among the twenty-six authors who reflected on the teaching and learning experiences emanated from the Urban Seminar, most were professors. Other contributors included school district personnel, such as human resource director, regional superintendent, principals and cooperating teachers.

Norris Square Community Center facilitators also shared their perspective. All faculty members who edited papers served on its Editorial Board. This book was published by the National Social Science Associations (NSSA) two weeks before the Urban Education Conference. It was just in time to be distributed at the conference to all participating teachers, professors, and administrators as an urban education resource book. After the hard copy of the book was printed, the publisher also made it into a CD book of the same title, and its digital version is available on NSSA's website.

While the first book was mainly a product of faculty and other facilitators, *Our Stories in Philadelphia,* the current one, has demonstrated more extensive faculty and student collaborations. This book employs the time honored story telling as a major genre of the book to encourage more faculty and student participation. The book was initiated by a professor, supported by faculty coordinators, and then communicated to all participants. At Urban Seminar 2009's final professional development meeting at Philadelphia, while waiting for Mayer Nutter of Philadelphia to make a speech, the professor announced the project to all 500 students. She encouraged all participants to write their most memorable stories they experienced during the Urban Seminar, which, in her words, would make readers laugh, cry and think. Hopefully these stories would also make leadership and the public take positive actions for urban and all students.

Many professors and students were excited by the initiative. Twenty students signed up their story writing intentions on the spot. Later, fifty more participants responded to the call. When the papers were returned, campus faculty coordinators served as preliminary editors for these stories. They screened and edited student stories and then recommended them to the major editors of the book. Eventually, 35 papers were selected to be included in the book. All faculty members who edited student papers serve on the Editorial Board.

Figure 5.4 Professors from 20 universities meeting at
Philadelphia

The Urban Education Conference and the books above are
just a few examples of numerous collaborations among faculty.
This much appreciated collaboration not only made the planning,
budgeting, and execution of the Urban Conference and book
publications easier, it also greatly enhanced the bonding among
faculty. These collaborations and bonding, energized by the faculty's
dedication to urban education especially after they witnessed the
huge program impact, are some of the real driving forces that have
enabled the success of the Urban Seminars for the last 18 years.
Dr. Connie Armitage of California University of PA highlighted
this collaboration and bonding sentiment best in her message to all
faculty coordinators when she missed the Urban Seminar 2009:

To All My Faculty Friends,
    I have always felt blessed to have the opportunity to
work with all of you on the Philadelphia Urban Seminar.
Now, the care and concern you have shown towards me

has reminded me of the wonderful gift of having good people in my life. You are truly a special group of which I feel privileged to be a part. You have enriched my life in so many ways. Although I missed this year's Urban Seminar, I have already heard from my students that it was a wonderful experience. It is amazing how each year the comments are the same: "One of the best experiences of my college career" and "Everyone should be required to take this course." I was not surprised to hear these comments and hear the enthusiasm of the students. Let me congratulate everyone on another success of our Urban Seminar.

Most sincerely,

Connie

Dr. Armitage's letter says it all. This collaboration and bonding, which underlines the success of the Urban Conference, the Books and the entire Urban Seminar, will always be cherished among all participating faculty coordinators of the Philadelphia Urban Seminar.

(Julie Q. Bao is a professor at Shippensburg University.)

Chapter Six

For Urban and All Students

This final chapter of stories looks at the Urban Seminar from several perspectives and looks forward to the future of the program. In her article, Professor Claire Verden sums up the experiences as a combination of plenty of running around, a lot of laughter, hard work, and sharing memorable moments. She points out that the lasting characteristic is the change in attitude that she sees in her students as they grow both as future teachers and as global citizens. Reflecting on her journey from being a teacher in the School District of Philadelphia to being an instructor in the Urban Seminar, Professor Lynnette Mawhinney recalls how her passion for teaching and making a difference is being passed on to her Urban Seminar students. She tells of how her students created individually handmade gifts for each student in their classroom, thus demonstrating their appreciation for their students, and perhaps more importantly, their passion for teaching urban students. In that moment, Professor Mawhinney realized that coming home had brought her a full circle. The Urban Seminar invigorated the passion in her college students, but it also reinvigorated her in the process.

Recruiting students to participate in the Urban Seminar is the theme of the article by Professor Jannis Floyd. She emphasizes that recruiting efforts highly rely on former participants to provide testimony to the value of the Urban Seminar. These students are convincing as they describe how they have been able to use their Urban Seminar experiences in other classes as well as in their personal lives. Professor Floyd notes that the long-term benefit is the ability of students to make a personal connection between their university coursework and real students, parents and community members.

A distinctive component of the Philadelphia Urban Seminar is involvement of participants in community improvement projects. Reed Davaz-McGowan describes how Philadelphia Urban Seminar students have become involved as volunteers assisting with large-scale projects within one inner-city community. She describes how the partnership between the Urban Seminar and the neighborhood association has helped the community, but also has provided the students with many rich examples of Puerto Rican culture.

An interesting and surprising aspect of the Urban Seminar emerged when a dozen students, and their university teachers, from The Netherlands joined the program. The continuing participation by students from Rotterdam offered a unique perspective on the Urban Seminar, which is described by two of the instructors, Rosa Rodrigues and Els Fonville-Kuhlmann. Their participation in the program challenged their images of the United States, perceptions of American education, their expectations of schools in low income areas, and teaching in urban schools. They identified several themes that characterized the teaching in these Philadelphia schools which they noted are highly valued in Dutch urban schools.

The international perspective is extended in the article by Professor Nurun Begum, who compares her early experiences in urban settings in her native Bangladesh to the situation in Philadelphia. Professor Begum explores several themes, all of which are stories about life, suffering, and hope. She notes that these stories bring tears, give us pain, and warn us to be strong and dedicated. From this strength and dedication we can build a foundation of hope—hope for urban children.

In the closing article, Julie Bao and George Bieger explain the current status of the program, use faculty testimony on the Urban Seminar to emphasize the importance of the urban education cause, use a model to illustrate the five major characteristics of the Urban Seminar, and sum up the current status and significance of the program.

Changes in Latitudes, Changes in Attitudes
Claire Verden

It's these changes in latitudes, changes in attitudes
Nothing remains quite the same
With all of our running and all of our cunning
If we couldn't laugh we would all go insane
Jimmy Buffett, 1977

I am inspired by the lyrics of the great Jimmy Buffett when I think about the Philadelphia Urban Seminar and in particular the students from West Chester University who participate in this program. Having just completed my third summer of the Urban Seminar with my undergraduate students, it is their change in attitude that I am continually amazed by and driven by to want to continue offering this wonderful program to future teachers. Each year West Chester offers this program as part of a special education block of classes whereby 28 undergraduate special education students take their field course as a part of the Urban Seminar and then come back to campus for a two-course follow up; they earn a total of nine credits for the three course block.

Initially many students see this opportunity as a way to get three courses out of the way and either catch up or get ahead during the summer months. What they are not prepared for is the evolutionary process that they will go though during their two weeks working and living in Philadelphia. By the middle of the fall semester I am questioned repeatedly by folks interested in the program for the following summer; they have heard by word of mouth about the program even though there is no official advertising done on campus. Generally we start an "interest list" for participation and then take a break for a few months!

In early spring we will start to do some of our administrative duties; order mini-vans to transport our students, coordinate with IUP regarding the number of students we will bring and the type of field placement classroom they will need, and start to gather our course materials. Then it is time for the fun to begin: the initial student meeting! After a room is scheduled for our meeting (not an easy endeavor) and a time is selected that fits MOST schedules (even less of an easy endeavor) we all get together for the first time. At this first meeting will be students that I have already had in class and know well, as well as students that I am meeting for the first time. In general there will be 28 students who are registered for the course and possibly more who are on a wait list.

The first shock for some of the students is that they will be living at La Salle University for the two-week span and will not be able to go home each night; shock and horror appear on many faces! At this point there are usually a few who will drop out, not realizing that this is a full time 24-hour per day commitment for two weeks. Others are better informed and feel able to go with the flow. We go over the mundane items that need to be discussed; bring professional work clothes, pack a lunch each day, bring a laptop, if you want your own pillow and comforter bring it along and the fact that you will need to bring a portable light and a fan is always a good idea.

I can start to get a sense for how the whole program will go once we get to Philadelphia based on the types of questions that I am asked at this initial meeting. "Is there a T.V., I need to watch the final episode of Law and Oder?" —this question does not bode well for full participation in the Urban Seminar! "I need my coffee, should I bring my own coffee pot?" —possible implications for a person who is very needy or possibly just a person who knows exactly what they need each day to do a good job! "Do I have to stay over the weekend or can I go home for my family cookout?" —You need to fully participate in this program to get the most out of it; if you only partially participate you will only get partial benefit.

You get a true measure of a student's future aspiration to be a good teacher by the ways in which they handle the very first day of the program. Do they have patience? If they can cooperate with 500 of their closest peers to move into the dormitories all at the same time, then yes, you have a good future as a patient teacher! Are they a flexible person? If they can agree to a change in plans without complaining, then yes, their future as a teacher looks rosy! When they are tired, hungry and need to use the bathroom can they wait while one more speaker finishes up what they are saying? Is this not the true measure of a good teacher; when the call of nature is upon you and you have to wait?

Many of the issues that students are concerned about before they participate in the program are very real fears and are typically shared by their families. Their families worry about them being in the City and teaching in an urban school setting that is unfamiliar to them. The majority of the students that participate in the program from West Chester are female, Caucasian and grew up in the suburbs. The Philadelphia that they know is to visit sites of interest downtown or to go out to dinner. They are not comfortable being "the minority" and feel on edge when immersed in a culture different to their own. Many question whether they will be safe during the two-weeks and if the neighborhood schools that they will go into will be like those portrayed in the media with metal detectors and police officers. As one student wrote in her journal "I have no real experience with teaching in a diverse classroom or even being a student in one, so as of now, I am more fearful of the unknown than anything else."

Of course all new experiences can be daunting and there is only so much reassuring that the professors can do before the students go into the schools and find out for themselves. After the very first day in the schools, I start to sing Jimmy Buffett in my head! Indeed, *It is these changes in latitudes, changes in attitudes, Nothing remains quite the same.* Although technically the change in latitude from West Chester Pennsylvania to Philadelphia Pennsylvania is only a matter of 39 minutes of arc, (basically this means that we are on the same line of latitude) but it is the change in attitude that is immeasurable!

As soon as students return from their schools and we head into our evening seminar sessions I hear statements like "My biggest fear and concern had been my safety within and around the school. Having spent a full day there, this concern has become practically obsolete." My students forget about their fears and start to build immediate relationships with the children in the classrooms; they can put a face to urban education! Not only do these children look different than they do but many of them do not speak English as a first language and come from economically struggling families. This only seems to add to the power of their experience as one student explained in her journal, "I was able to put aside the differences in culture, race, home structure, socioeconomic status, and language. What remained were children whose differences helped bring life into the classroom and made them the unique individuals they are."

I was able to see so much change in some of my students that is hard to quantify! Some students had previously been in my classes back on campus for a traditional semester long field experience; I thought I knew them well! The same students complaining about lack of access to coffee, the small dormitory rooms, and yes the mice (you must have heard about the mice?) were now showing empathy and a resilience that I did not think they possessed. Professors too make judgments and have pre-conceived ideas about how their students will respond to certain situations; I am proud to say that I was completely and utterly wrong in many cases. Instead of complaining about the mice in the dorms I heard them saying "This must be what it is like for some of my students, I can put up with it for two weeks if they can put up with it everyday of their lives."

During the middle weekend of the program, which this year happened to fall over Memorial Day Weekend, each University commits to a community service project in one of the neighboring communities. For West Chester University it was the Norris Square Neighborhood Project. We worked with some other university groups and with the Norris Square Community Group to spend the full day Saturday cleaning up the park and surrounding areas. This was a day for my students to really get down and dirty as they weeded, moved dirt and mulch, created garden beds, picked up trash from the streets and prepared food for the lunch picnic in the park. By afternoon we had many very tired, dirty and sunburned students but the fun was just beginning! We participated in a Children's Festival where we set up booths for the young children in the neighborhood to come by and create necklaces, get their faces painted, join in many games and activities and just get to know each other on a more personal basis. One story that I remember from the festival was a young lady about 12 years old who did not speak English. My students did not speak Spanish so there was an immediate communication challenge! This was easily resolved when they worked collaboratively to make a necklace using alphabet letters that spelled out the young lady's name; even without a common language they were getting to know each other.

At the end of the two-weeks in the schools on the last day of their field experience, when only the week before many students were counting the days until they could go home, many of the undergraduates are tearful and saying how much they love this experience and of course the children with whom they have come into contact. They cannot fathom that only two-weeks in a classroom can garner such strong emotions as they have to leave the school and go back to West Chester. As one student in her journal entry explains: "In the end I realized that no matter where the students came from, what kind of life they lived, or what color their skin was they are still kids. Kids that need teachers like me to take the challenge, accept who they are, and work to support their individual needs. I have developed a comfortable feeling and realized that I could be a teacher in an urban setting."

As we gather for one final time as a group, students eagerly share all that they have seen and all that they want to do in the future with regard to their teaching careers. Many leave feeling that teaching in an urban environment is something that they want and plan to do. Others feel that it is now an option that they might consider depending on their life circumstances. After three summers and over 75 students I have yet to have anyone tell me that this is absolutely not for them and that all of their pre-conceived notions about urban education are true. The power of this experience is hard to measure and quantify with statistical data alone; it is the anecdotal and journal entry information that proves to me that this can be a life changing experience for my students. Their actions speak for themselves as many go on to request an urban placement for their student teaching experience and several have been hired by the School District of Philadelphia as special education teachers. One student journal entry best sums up this powerful experience:

> I have seen some changes within myself after spending my two weeks at the Urban Seminar. I have definitely seen a change in my attitude. I have a different way of looking at these students and their intentions…I also saw some changes in my comfort level in an urban environment. I cannot stress enough how much I learned from this experience, and I am so glad that I was able to experience it.

Do you hear the strains of Jimmy Buffett as I do?

> *It's these changes in latitudes, changes in attitudes*
> *Nothing remains quite the same*
> *With all of our running and all of our cunning*
> *If we couldn't laugh we would all go insane*
> Jimmy Buffett, 1977

We did plenty of running around during the two weeks and yes, there was some cunning involved! There was a lot of laughter throughout the whole experience from the first day when we could not get into a local high school for our first meeting and 500 people waited on the sidewalk, to the last night when people shared some of their memorable moments from the program. But it is the change in attitude that continues to strike me as I see my students grow in immense ways as both future teachers and become more global citizens.

(Claire Verden is an assistant professor at West Chester University.)

Coming Home: An Urban Teacher's Return as a Professor
Lynnette Mawhinney

"Alright, I hope you all have a wonderful time teaching today!" "Thanks, Dr. Mawhinney. See you this afternoon," said Martin as he shut the van door. As I sat behind the driver's seat of a 15-passenger van, I was watching as my college students crossed the street into the Philadelphia elementary school. I was flooded with various emotions as I watched them enter the school on their way to being urban teachers. Will they see the beauty in teaching in an urban school district? Will they struggle with classroom management? Interestingly, these are all the same questions I harbored when I was first teaching. It was only a mere ten years ago that I was in the same position as my college students, entering an urban school as a teacher for the first time.

The Beginning

After teaching high school English in New Jersey for a year, I decided to teach in the School District of Philadelphia. I always saw myself as an urban teacher, so I took the opportunity when it came. It was an $8,000 pay cut from my previous teaching position, but I was committed to teaching in an urban area. The job opportunity aligned with my vision of my career. The added benefit was that the commute would be less strenuous since I already lived in Philadelphia, at that time, for the last two years.

So after extensive curriculum planning over the summer, the first day of teaching in Philadelphia was here. The day started off like any other day. I woke up, took a shower, and grabbed a protein bar for breakfast. The difference on this day was the butterflies in my stomach. The mix of excitement and nervousness were all playing a tap dance routine in my mind. This routine continued on my drive to the school. As I approached my destination, I found myself circling around the streets of North Philadelphia trying to look for parking. I finally found a parking spot next to an abandoned building that would moonlight as a crack house. Adjacent to the building was my new school. I entered the doors of my new place of employment with anticipation, passion, and naïveté.

Only a few short months after teaching, the comments started coming. Friends and even strangers would say, "I do not know how you can teach in Philadelphia" or "Those kids have to be rough" or the classic line, "I would never teach in Philadelphia in a million years." These are the same comments I still hear on a regular basis. Yet, my experience teaching in Philadelphia did not jade me like most people expected. It did quite the opposite. My teaching experience fueled my anticipation and passion for teaching urban youth. My only loss was my naïveté about the urban school system. Over time I realized the extensive politics that were interconnected in the system that I was too naïve to previously notice. Thus, I tried my best to abstain from getting too caught up into the politics of education. I was content on keeping my focus on my classroom and students.

After teaching in the district for a couple of years, my sense of urgency to conduct good work within urban education was furthered with an opportunity to work full-time on a Ph.D. in Urban Education at Temple University. I took this opportunity as a chance to learn more about the current research behind urban education, and to use that knowledge back into my high school classroom. Since I was offered an assistantship at my university, I had to temporary leave the high school classroom. The good news was that Temple University was in the same section of the city as my high school, so it provided a chance to visit my students.

Although I was provided this great opportunity to further my education, leaving the School District of Philadelphia was very difficult for me. I often had anxiety thinking about the obvious questions: Will my students feel like I am abandoning them? By going back to school, am I just becoming another statistic of urban teachers' leaving? In some ways, the answer is "yes" to all of the above. While I often went back to see my students and still currently keep in touch with them, some students did feel abandoned by me going back to school. Even though I was pursuing my Ph.D., in some ways I do factor into the statistics of urban teachers leaving within the first five years of teaching. On the other hand, I knew that I was using this time in higher education in order to strengthen my pedagogy and practice in urban schools.

The assistantship I received at Temple University was to teach two educational methods courses. Initially, I was not all that interested in teaching higher education. I thought these classes would just be a bunch of college students going through the motions. I immediately found out I was wrong. In fact, these students were the same as my urban high school students. They were coming from the same school district, and they needed the same scaffolds and supports. Moreover, I realized my impact on urban education was bigger at the postsecondary level. At the high school level, I could influence and have a positive impact on 100 students within one school year. At the higher education level, I could impact 100 teachers who are then going to positively influence their 100 students. Thus, the influence on urban education is greater at the higher education level. I immediately felt that I could do more good and provide my skills to urban education more effectively in teacher education.

While completing my Ph.D., the City certainly changed. The crack house where I used to park my car was turned into high-end loft apartments. The murder rate in the City was on the rise. The CEO of the school district changed hands. My status as a teacher in the district may have changed like the evolving city, but I would soon find that the Urban Seminar would provide an opportunity to lead me back into the School District of Philadelphia.

The Urban Seminar: Providing the Way Back Home

As an urban teacher, I am very committed to teacher education having experiences to promote urban teachers. This was part of the reason why I decided to teach at Lincoln University after graduating with my Ph.D. Located in the middle of rural Amish Country, Lincoln University is America's first Historically Black University. The majority of students come from the surrounding urban areas: Philadelphia, New York City, Baltimore, Washington, D.C. and the like. Furthermore, a number of my former ninth grade students from Philadelphia attended Lincoln University when I started my job there, which was a nice perk. More importantly, I would have the opportunity to work with urban youth at an institution committed to the urban students.

Upon entering Lincoln University, I realized there was a glitch in the system. Since most of our students were educated in urban schools, most of our teacher education graduates start their careers in urban schools. Yet at the time of my arrival, none of the students' field experiences in the teacher education program involved urban schools. When this issue was discovered, I decided to go to a conference in Harrisburg concerning urban education. It was at this conference that I met Dr. Larry Vold, the head facilitator of the Urban Seminar. The Urban Seminar was a great opportunity to get the Lincoln University pre-service teachers involved with urban education. This was a unique experience that spoke to all the needs of our education majors.

I also realized that the Urban Seminar would place me on the other side of the classroom. Here I was, a former School District of Philadelphia teacher about to enter back into the district. However, I was not going back as a teacher but as a guide to other prospective teachers.   I was coming home with a new role.

Ultimately, the Urban Seminar provided a chance for me to witness the evolution of urban teachers while looking from the outside. In two weeks, I saw a passion fueled in my Lincoln University pre-service teachers that I had never seen before. They were committed to African-American youth like themselves. They were committed to the idea of change in the urban classroom. They were committed to teaching in the urban school district.

This commitment and dedication to the urban students was solidified on the last night of the Urban Seminar. Around 2:00am I received a phone call from one of my students, "Hey, if you are still around, come to our building and see what we are making!" As I entered their building, most of my students were out in the hallway. Scissors, construction paper, stickers, and pictures were scattered on the floor. My pre-service teachers had decided to create individually handmade gifts for each student in their classroom. This was their way of demonstrating their appreciation for their students, but it was also a tangible depiction of their passion for urban students.

In that moment I saw myself in my students. I saw myself, ten years earlier, staying up late to create fun and engaging activities for my ninth graders. I was reminded of not sleeping one night in order to handwrite personalized messages to each of my high school students. I recollect my initial passion for urban teaching which was reflecting back at me as my Lincoln University students, now urban teachers, were creating these gifts. In this moment, coming home had brought me full circle. The Urban Seminar invigorated the passion in my college students, but it also reinvigorated me in the process.

(Lynnette Mawhinney is an assistant professor at The College of New Jersey.)

Recruiting for the Urban Seminar
Jannis V. Floyd

Participating in the Urban Seminar has been a rewarding and challenging experience for me as a teacher educator. It is rewarding because we have an opportunity to provide our pre-service teachers with a quality experience in a different geographic region, with individuals from diverse backgrounds, experiences, and languages;

and opportunities to meet students from across the state. Yet, recruiting students for the Seminar and leading them through the program pose special challenges for our university. Mansfield University is a small rural liberal arts university located at the cross roads of Route 15 and Route 6 in the scenic mountains of the Northern Tier of Pennsylvania. The university and the community of Mansfield have a long shared history spanning over one hundred and fifty years. We have approximately 3,500 students which makes us the second smallest of the 14 universities in the Pennsylvania State System of Higher Education.

We were invited to participate in the Urban Seminar six years ago. When the email arrived, requesting volunteers to coordinate the program on our campus, I was eager to participate. This would be a wonderful opportunity for our students to experience diversity beyond what our region has to offer and for our education program to make contacts in order to expand our field experience placement opportunities. It was a conscious decision in the beginning to keep this program small. The maximum number with one faculty member is set at 15 students. We wanted to get to know each student, observe the students in their school settings and participate in historical and cultural activities with the group. Each year as a group we take a tour of the city, have a cheese steak meal, a group meal at a restaurant of the students' choosing, and participant in local cultural and historical events such as museum exhibits and salsa lessons.

The first year, recruiting was a learning experience. Flyers were sent out to all education programs along with information about the program. An information session was scheduled. Dr. Vold, the Head Coordinator of the Urban Seminar met with me earlier and shared the goals, information about program activities, housing and costs. I was ready, but nobody showed up. Undaunted I tried again—flyers, talking it up among my colleagues. As a result, several students came to the second meeting. Some students later contacted me expressing their interest but only two signed up. So that first year we had only two Mansfield students that participated.

The next year I scheduled more information sessions and varied the day of the week and time of day. For the next couple of years I added refreshments to the agenda. That brought in more interested individuals and more participants—we now fill the van.

There have been several major areas of concern in recruiting participants for the Urban Seminar at Mansfield University. A major difficulty in recruiting has been money or lack of—Many of our students must work in the summer to help support their schooling and families. The program provided a grant for housing but students must pay for tuition and fees, the administrative fee, food (only a few meals are provided) and spending money. For the last three years we have been holding bake sales/Krispy Cream to help supplement or cover the cost of group activities. I have applied for and received several professional development grants that have included the cost of the van, the city tour and several meals. However, without these extra sources of funding, our students would find it much more difficult to attend.

Scheduling is another area of concern for our students wishing to participate in the Urban Seminar. The dates of the program have fallen in one of our regular summer sessions. We must compete with courses that meet general education and program requirements. The urban seminar course is a free elective. The experiences are invaluable to the students and benefit them in their teaching but it is not a required course. Hopefully this can be changed.

Fear is often brought up as the major concern—fear for safety, fear of traveling to someplace new and different, concerns about ability to teaching. I am often asked by students and parents who call, Is it safe, Philadelphia is a metropolitan city, we hear on the news about all the crime? I share with the students pictures of the dorm complex where we will be staying and tell them that there is a 24-hour monitoring system and no one enters without a keycard. You need to understand that the Mansfield is rural and folks know who you are here—our closest city in PA is Williamsport, and it is almost an hour away to the south.

Mansfield, in distance, is closer to Corning and Elmira, NY but none of these cities have the size and diversity of Philadelphia. Some students have not participated because of their concerns or fears about the city. For our students who have participated I see those concern or fears addressed in their journals only for the first few days of the experience. Once they have been to the dorm, to the neighborhood grocery store, had their first day at school they begin to focus on the teaching and learning experience—theirs and their students.

Our best recruiting tool has been our students who have participated in the Urban Seminar. After the first three years we have had an increase in the interest in the Urban Seminar and in students who participated in the experience. I believe that is due for the most part to our students who come back to campus and share their experiences, both positive and negative, with other students. Flyers get the information out to our education majors but seeing pictures and hearing from actual participants is our most effective recruiting tool. We have a banner and a quilt hanging outside my office that were created by Urban Seminar participants—both include photos of their activities as well as drawing created by the students in their classrooms. The 2009 group has a picture book that collates their experiences. All of these items help in our recruitment efforts for the Urban Seminar.

Our Mansfield students have been able to use their Urban Seminar experiences in their other education classes and in their personal lives—some have remained in contact with their cooperating teachers; they are more open and receptive to meeting new people and trying new activities. They have been able to connect much better the multicultural and diversity instruction provided in their education courses to real students, parents and community members.

(Jannis V. Floyd is an associate professor in Mansfield University.)

The Spirit of the Urban Seminar throughout the Year
Reed Davaz McGowan

The mission of Norris Square Neighborhood Project (NSNP) is to nurture and actively involve neighborhood children and their families in learning responsibilities for self, culture, community, and environment. NSNP is a community-driven, bilingual environmental and cultural learning center. It provides residents of the predominantly Latino Norris Square neighborhood of North Philadelphia with quality youth leadership development programs including after-school childcare and summer camp childcare, an entrepreneurial teen silk screening program, programs supporting and empowering neighborhood women, community gardening/ neighborhood beautification efforts and community education classes in technology and English as a second language. NSNP programs and gardens aim at connecting people with Puerto Rican, Mexican, Dominican and other cultures.

The history of NSNP began in a small row house located at 2141 North Howard Street, in the West Kensington section of North Philadelphia. In 1973, Natalie Kempner, a local fifth grade teacher, and Dr. Helen Loeb, a professor at Eastern University of Pennsylvania, founded NSNP. The two women collaborated with a dedicated group of volunteer teachers, artists and community residents to create environmental education that was culturally relevant to and protective of the children living in a section of Philadelphia that was notorious for its deadly drug culture. Over more than three decades, the agency's work has grown in scope and impact as the predominately Latino community around it has expanded and flourished. The environmental and cultural education programs of NSNP have helped transform the surrounding community and the lives of Norris Square residents.

The Philadelphia Urban Seminar's involvement with the Norris Square Neighborhood Project since the mid 1990's yields long lasting benefits for the Norris Square community as a result of the weekend-long concentrated visit to NSNP by several hundred pre-service teachers, and the two-week service that many of the college students conduct in neighborhood schools. For the weekend of service, the Norris Square community transforms with the college students partnering with community residents to create a positive presence in the neighborhood.

Physical changes occur within the neighborhood. Students clean the streets, paint park structures and do major upkeep projects on NSNP's six gardens. Grupo Motivos, NSNP's Puerto Rican women's collective cooks meals for the students, offering many of them their first taste of Puerto Rican food. Youth in NSNP's After School Program performs traditional Puerto Rican Bomba dances with community artists, Familia Rojas. The special opportunities afforded by NSNP's partnership with the Urban Seminar allows for a mutually beneficial sharing of cultures and backgrounds. College students experience Puerto Rican culture and community residents work side by side with young people from varying backgrounds.

After the Urban Seminar ends each year, there is hope to maintain the relationships. Common understanding between such different backgrounds lingers and many students affected positively by the experience express a desire to return to the Norris Square community. Following the 2008 Urban Seminar, NSNP was approached by Philadelphia Biblical University (PBU) and Cabrini College, two higher education institutions that participate annually in the Urban Seminar. Cabrini College faculty and students have returned to NSNP's gardens to share the cultural experience with people new to Philadelphia and the work of NSNP, while PBU students have had continuous presence in NSNP's After School Program. NSNP offers a low-cost, quality After School Program for students ages 6-18, which focuses on environmental, arts and cultural learning. NSNP's program provides quality traditional arts and crafts instruction including cooking, visual and performing arts focusing on Puerto Rican culture along with academic enrichment and literacy development. The program connects youth to the environment through gardening and neighborhood beautification, while instilling values and encouraging civic engagement. NSNP emphasizes youth leadership, intergenerational mentoring by older community members and constituency-led decision making in these programs. The oldest youth, ages 14-18, plan and operate an entrepreneurial silk-screening project called "Prodigies."

PBU students have regularly volunteered as a part of their ministry and service within NSNP's After School Program. The college students tutor and mentor program youth across all ages ranging from Kindergarten to 12th grades. Responsibilities include reading to youth, helping with homework, assisting youth with special project completion and aiding NSNP's program staff with classroom management and project-based learning activities. This longitudinal service has provided NSNP with a consistent presence within its programming of pre-service teachers which has not only contributed immensely to the infrastructure of NSNP's programs, but has created bonds between youth and college mentors that are not easily found in most settings.

Figure 6.1 Reading at Norris Square Children's Festival

NSNP hopes to maintain its relationship with PBU and Cabrini College and welcomes other schools wishing to develop continued relationships that occur after the weekend-long Urban Seminar event in May. Through this partnership, NSNP helps to prepare pre-service teachers in an urban environment while gaining invaluable service from the volunteers. NSNP's involvement with these schools lasts far beyond that weekend of service; and the impression left on participants of all backgrounds extends to the community in many ways for a long time. Nearly 60 former Urban Seminar students have gone on to teach in community schools. It is NSNP's hope that their work with NSNP has better prepared them to work with Latino youth in North Philadelphia.

Urban Seminar's Involvement in NSNP's Gardens

Over the last decade and a half, the collaboration between Norris Square Neighborhood Project and the Philadelphia Urban Seminar has contributed greatly to NSNP's six gardens. NSNP staff, Grupo Motivos members, volunteers and Urban Seminar partners annually prepare *Las Parcelas, Villa Africana Colobó, Raices, Jardín de Paz, El Batey* and *the Butterfly Garden* for the garden season. While the gardens are now the highlight of the neighborhood during the late spring, summer and early fall, the gardens evolved from less than beautiful origins.

Once values of neighborhood house property (from West Susquehanna to West Dauphin, and from North Palethorp to North Second Street) began deteriorating in the late 1970's and 1980's, many places became areas of drug sales and prostitution. Some of them literally fell down in front of other residents' eyes. After these houses disappeared, empty lots blighted the neighborhood where other community members were trying to carry on their lives. The predominately Puerto Rican community witnessed outside companies dumping demolition debris and construction waste into these empty lots.

Community residents, spearheaded by Grupo Motivos, established a series of remarkable green oases on those once abandoned lots or heroin drug points by using their Puerto Rican culture as the foundation for their greening projects. These projects began by NSNP securing state funds to first fence in lots in this area and grew into the gardens by the dreams of community resident Tomasita Romero, a longtime NSNP volunteer and member of Grupo Motivos, to see trees in her neighborhood. The trees, now large and statuesque presences in the gardens, led to other plants and artworks being envisioned and placed into the gardens by Iris Brown, NSNP's visionary gardener. Iris yearned to create slices of Puerto Rico in North Philadelphia to bring beauty to the neighborhood that was so rich with culture and remind community members of their tropical patria.

The culturally-themed gardens, still maintained by community elders, act as a community cultural center. The gardens are a space to share organically grown foods, oral traditions, stories and to weave generations of community members together. Pennsylvania Horticultural Society awards annual prizes for the culturally-themed gardens and they are used as models for other urban gardening programs. Aside from being renowned for their work in NSNP's award-winning gardens, the women of Grupo Motivos have developed an intergenerational model of educating neighborhood youth. Grupo Motivos was founded by its members in 1990 in response to the need for local women to support each other and their community. The members are 15 to 75 years old and Grupo Motivos membership has ranged from 5 to 16 women. Through the determined efforts of Grupo Motivos, NSNP has helped community members of all ages take an active role in cleaning up their neighborhood and strengthening civic culture. The women of Grupo Motivos have worked diligently to support other local women and girls throughout the last 18 years. Through work in NSNP's gardens, community service projects and the Grupo Motivos' catering business, women are empowered to bring skills to table. Grupo Motivos members have a wealth of cultural knowledge, urban gardening, agricultural knowledge, and the ability to cater Puerto Rican meals. Grupo Motivos has empowered many women who have faced significant difficulties in life due to immigration to the United States, poverty, lack of other resources, limited knowledge of English, and domestic violence.

Iris Brown, NSNP's Garden Coordinator, has worked closely with the women's collective as both a member and a coordinator of activities and endeavors. She has directed the garden projects over the years and has led the two most recent additions of an African garden, *Villa Africana Colobó*, and a new portion of *Las Parcelas* dedicated to children called *Quiquiriqui*. Both of these projects have had significant support from the Urban Seminar, along with NSNP's other gardens.

In an interview in 2008, Iris discussed the development of the African Garden. For her, Villa Africana Colobó is a dream come true. The African garden examines the lesser studied and discussed African root within Puerto Rican culture that is mixed with Spanish and indigenous Taíno blood. For many years, Iris Brown thought about that space and thought about making an African garden. When considering the gardens, it is extremely important that NSNP uses its gardens in many different ways. In this neighborhood, there is a lack of resources to explore and learn about Puerto Rican roots in Africa. Puerto Ricans are part of Africans. She acknowledges that it is not written in books, but it something that she sees, something that she feels. When people here are working with children, it is necessary for them to learn about their culture, who they are, how to obtain education, how to be good citizens, and how to build relationships with those who share their culture and those who do not. The Story Telling Room in the African Garden is a space to tell stories, sad, happy, and educational. Through these stories, community members and others will learn about each other and what is going on in this community. The African Garden is a place to learn about gardening, plants, organic vegetables, herbs, and flowers. It is a place to cook, play drums, and dance—a perfect combination.

The creation of the garden seemed logical to Iris Brown. NSNP had one garden about the Taínos, El Batey, and Las Parcelas is mostly about Puerto Rican culture, although many things go on there. One garden needed to be dedicated to Africa. When people say that they are going to Villa Africana Colobó, she wanted people to know that they would be celebrating and learning about Africa. The garden became a reality by dreaming. Every day, the dream was fresh in Iris' mind, so she kept writing down the plans that she imagined. Once Iris was having the dream everyday, it was so vivid that she could smell the flowers and the herbs, and see the colors and the designs. It became real to her. She was excited and inspired by articles, patterns, and meeting people who knew about African villages. They supported her idea. Iris was surprised to find so many people interested in helping make it happen, because she had never heard anyone in this community or really anywhere talk about an African garden. Pennsylvania Horticultural Society, Dr. Vold's Urban Seminar, M-Fuge, Temple University students, the Philadelphia Mural Arts Program, NSNP's Summer Day Camp children, Jim Shields, Roberto Rojas, and of course, Tomasita Romero, all made it possible.

Iris continues to dream about the garden and says that she wants to have many visitors coming to the garden from different cultures with activities and workshops, too. She wants to be able to cook with herbs and vegetables that are grown right there. Her dream is to cook with African men and women. She believes that when one dreams, and if the dream comes true, one would want to share it. Hopefully, it will inspire and start a *dialogo*. Iris wants the garden to provoke so that people will start thinking and researching.

Iris has continued the development of the gardens by the creation of *Quiquiriqui*, a children's garden, in *Las Parcelas*. During the Urban Seminar of 2009, with funds provided primarily by the Urban Seminar and Pennsylvania Horticultural Society, Earth Partnership and individual donations, NSNP was able to dedicate a portion of its largest garden to the instruction and programming for neighborhood youth. The impetus of the Urban Seminar gave Iris the opportunity to plan and dream for the new garden. Iris gathered community artists and developed a plan for garden beds that looked like trains and a fence made out of large wooden crayons. Kelsey Harro, NSNP's Volunteer Coordinator, helped Iris to coordinate students to paint the fence in the course of the Urban Seminar while Iris led other painting, construction, weeding and gardening projects in support of *QuiquiriQui*.

The development of these two gardens would not have been possible without partnership with the Urban Seminar. The Urban Seminar provides volunteers to take on large-scale projects within the community and NSNP's other gardens, major undertakings that prepare the gardens for the rest of the garden season. This partnership has allowed NSNP's gardens to expand and flourish while continuing their presence as rich examples of Puerto Rican culture in the Norris Square community.

(Reed Davaz McGowan is the Director of Norris Square Neighborhood Project in Philadelphia.)

Our Experiences as Dutch Urban Teachers in Philadelphia
G.R. Rodrigues and E. Fonville-Kühlmann

Introduction

The University of Rotterdam is one of the three universities in Rotterdam (The Netherlands, Europe) and has approximately 30,000 students. About one-third of the students have an immigrant background. The university is divided into eleven schools and the School of Education consists of two departments: the Teacher Training for Secondary Education which facilitates about 2000 students, and the Teacher Training in Primary Education, called PABO, has about 1400 students (University, 2009).

This essay was written by lecturers from the PABO who guided the Dutch students in the Urban Seminar during the two weeks they were in Philadelphia. It is based on the diary texts of the students. In this chapter we first describe how we came to know about the Philadelphia Urban Seminar and why we decided to come to Philadelphia. We point out some of the similarities between our city of Rotterdam and Philadelphia and describe the students' experiences in the seminar. Finally, we identify some themes that emerged from the students' experiences in Philadelphia.

Learning about the Philadelphia Urban Seminar

The University of Rotterdam is a member of the European Teacher Education Network (ETEN) which was founded in 1988 and has 56 member institutions in 14 countries, several of which are in the United States (ETEN, 2009). During ETEN conferences, teacher educators from the PABO came into contact with professors from Indiana University of Pennsylvania (IUP), which had been organizing an Urban Seminar for years. In 2008, students from the PABO participated in this program for the first time with twelve third-year students (eleven from the Primary School Department, a student from the Secondary School Department) and two lecturers. In 2009 the participants included eleven third-year students plus a Spanish exchange student from an international class held at the PABO and three lecturers.

Why We Came to Philadelphia

For the PABO, it is important that there is room in the curriculum to acquire professional skills in an internationalized and inter-cultural environment and professional setting. In semester five, the third-year students work on the issue of *Educational disadvantages*. During this semester, they do an internship at a school and receive various educational classes on the subject. A decision was made to tailor this internship to the Philadelphia Urban Seminar during this fifth semester, for all interested third-year students. Participating in this program gives them a broader international perspective on education in economically disadvantaged neighborhoods. Students thus learn to adapt and develop their teaching methods and, in this way, they will be prepared to meet the challenge of teaching in a big city and choose to teach in urban schools.

Rotterdam and Philadelphia

As of September 1, 2009 The Netherlands had 16,536,017 inhabitants and approximately 20% of this population has an immigrant background. At the same time, the city of Rotterdam had 587,185 inhabitants and more than 168 nationalities (CBS, 2009). Thus, Rotterdam is also an immigrant city with a large variety of ethnic groups and social backgrounds. The diversity in the city of Rotterdam is a result of the city being an important harbor in The Netherlands. For a long time, employment was available to unskilled workers. The population in Rotterdam is also quite young, with almost one-quarter of the whole population being younger than 19 years old.

Rotterdam's average income is one of the lowest in The Netherlands. There are large differences among the city's neighborhoods. More than half of the primary school pupils from ethnic minorities in Rotterdam also have parents with low levels of education. Like Philadelphia Rotterdam has a significant teacher shortage in its urban schools. In The Netherlands, almost one-quarter of the students have a lag in their educational development. The reason for this lies in their social, economic, and cultural backgrounds. In The Netherlands, urban schools receive extra money to work with the economically disadvantaged (JOS, 2006).

Students' Experiences

Preparatory meetings were organized in The Netherlands to help the Dutch students prepare for the Urban Seminar in Philadelphia. The students were told that they were required to keep a journal to describe their experiences in Philadelphia. Later, they were asked to select interesting and inspiring passages from their journals that would address the following questions: 1. What is the responsibility and role of the teacher? 2. What do the children need? 3. How should you teach? 4. How does this program affect my vision regarding teaching in the city, and 5. What will I take back to The Netherlands concerning working in urban schools?

In the last two years, the PABO lecturers collected the journal passages and experiences of the Dutch students after they took part in the Urban Seminar program. In the following section, we have grouped the experiences of students into themes that are important for teaching in a multicultural school in an urban setting.

These themes are: *respect each other, personal awareness, education at school, high expectations, rest and regularity,* and *establish an inspiring learning environment.* The following sections are taken directly from the journals of the Dutch students whose names follow each excerpt.

Respect each other. It was my second day at my school when I was with the science teacher. The science teacher does not have a regular year group but teaches a different class every 45 minutes. In one of the second grade classes, the science teacher was telling her story about the food chain. After 20 minutes a girl raised her hand and she told the teacher that the girl behind her was saying 'white girl!' to her. At that moment the teacher was upset and came up with a story. She cut the shape of a girl out of a white paper and told the whole class the following story:

"There was a little girl who moved to another city. Her parents were not rich so she did not have enough money to wear fashionable clothes. So she went to a new school and on her first day she wore a funny dress. Her new classmates saw her and laughed because of her dress, and that really hurt her..."

At that moment the teacher wrinkled her leg.

"On her second day the girl came to school and her hair looked weird. When her classmates saw her they made fun of her. And that really hurt her..."

The teacher wrinkled another leg.

"On the third day at school she did not wear a strange dress and her hair did not look weird. So the children did not laugh. But when it

was play time and all the children were playing together she asked if she could play with them, but they said no! And that really hurt her..."

And the teacher wrinkled her arm.

"On the fourth day at school she looked normal and there was nothing wrong, but when a few kids were painting she asked them if she could join them, and again they said no! And that really hurt her..."

The teacher wrinkled her other arm.

"On Friday, her fifth day at school, there was lunch. All the kids in her class were sitting together and were laughing and making fun so she wanted to sit with them. She asked them if it was okay to sit with them and again they said no! And that really hurt her..."

Now the teacher wrinkled the rest of her body.

"The next week, on Monday, the girl was not at school. So the children asked their teacher where she was. The teacher explained that the girl was at home, that she did not want to come, because everyone was teasing her and that she was alone because the children in her class did not want to play with her. Everyone in her class was feeling bad because of the way they acted and they promised their teacher that they were sorry and they would not do it again. So the next day the little girl came back to school and the children played with her and she really felt welcome in her class, she made friends and was happy..."

The teacher ironed the paper girl, so you could see the shapes of the girl. But still you can see the folds of what has happened and done to her. With this story the teacher told the children that words or actions could hurt. Sometimes you can see it on the outside, but sometimes not. And when you hurt someone, you mark the person. And even when everything is okay and the person is really happy, they will forever carry the scars with them. (Jenice Böck, 2009)

For me, the first day immediately had me notice the way kids treated each other and approached me as a teacher. I noticed that the children showed respect for each other and to me. You do not have to expect a potty mouth as a teacher and if this happens again, it is instantly corrected. I also found the kids to be very polite. If they wanted to pass, for example, they said "excuse me." I think that the children, teachers and parents in The Netherlands can really learn from this. I believe the teachers in Holland tolerate far too much insolence and we must again teach children how to interact politely. (Emmelie van Leeuwen, 2008)

It is important to have mixed classes. With mixed classes children can learn better. There is a big problem with mixed classes though. The "student of color" may think that the white population is better. That can lead to problems in the class. So it is important to teach about other cultures. Give your lessons some color. That way, children learn about each other and will be able to understand one another. If you do not do that, your class will be separated into two groups, which makes it difficult for children to learn. It is definitely a challenge, but the result is very fulfilling to you as a teacher and the children. (Brenda Geestman, 2009)

Personal awareness. The Urban Seminar days always got better, step-by-step. The contact with the children went well and I increasingly got involved in their activities. I read and taught literacy and numeracy in small groups. We also had several meetings ourselves and I understood more of the purpose of this program. I also examined my own perspective. Where do I stand culture-wise? How flexible am I? What are my prejudices? How can I be more adaptable? After this contact, I saw that I need to focus more on myself instead of the group. I had my own views on cultural issues and a desire to be more open-minded. After I had done this, I found I gained better understanding of various approaches in the classroom and became more focused on my internship. I stopped comparing and put my prejudices aside. (Lydia Terlouw, 2008)

It is very important to be open-minded and thus have an open attitude towards new things. Do not hold on too tight to what you are used to. Try not to have a negative view, because very often there is a reason for the way children behave. You only find out if you dare to ask. Observe as much as possible and talk to the children. (Anouk van Broeckhuijsen, 2008)

Education at school. One day I asked my teacher: "What do you do if a child comes in late?" This was because a number of children were late every day. She gave the answer: "We are pleased that they are at school at all, so we do nothing." These children come from backgrounds where it is not always nice. Therefore, education in school is a key factor. There is structure, authority and there will be much attention paid to a safe learning environment. At first I thought the kids were very closed, given their traumatic experiences. But they have confided in me. At that point you are very close to the children. (Pricilla de Korte, 2008)

Saron was a boy in my kindergarten class. He liked to hang around me a lot. The other children did the same thing, but there was something special about Saron. During the times I taught he stared at me, as if he needed help. Even if we walked to the cafeteria or the gym he would always come to me to hold my hand. At a sudden point in time he came to me to ask for a private conversation. I asked my teacher, Mr. Solomon, if he was fine with this. He did not mind it at all. I took Saron from the group and he started staring at me again. I asked what he had to tell me. At that moment he took both my hands and asked if he would never see me again after this day. I looked at his cute face and saw that he hoped that I was going to tell him that we would see each other again. With pain in my heart I told him I was going back to The Netherlands not to return again. I saw the tears in his eyes and saw that he tried to stay strong and hide them from me. He grabbed something from his pocket, it was a toy car. He gave it to me and told me to take it home with me. I gave him a hug and continued my work. The hugs you get from these children are not regular hugs. They grab you really tight and do not want to let you go. (Angela Belder, 2009)

The thing that broke my heart though, was that Juan was crying the day I was leaving. I will never forget his face or the things he said. I never realized that children could get attached to you that quickly. I had only been there for two weeks and only did a couple of lessons and activities. I can understand why those kids need a stable base at school. They probably already have enough people outside the school who left them, so they cannot have people in the school leaving them too. It is their stable ground—the only thing that is going to be there every day, for five days a week. It is probably too disappointing for them to see that people are leaving them there too, because that is the image that they have of the world. They have no faith in it. How can you expect them to have good performance? I would definitely not. The responsibility that the teacher has in an urban school is much bigger then in one anywhere else. (Brenda Geestman, 2009)

High expectations. What I eventually will take with me to the urban schools in Rotterdam is the positive character of my teacher, her warmth and her love for teaching—believing in every child and caring for them while teaching. I do believe a child can achieve something if I have faith in him/her (Pygmalion Effect). If a teacher has high expectations of a child, the child will be challenged and will work harder to get to his/her goal. I have to keep in mind that children have different learning levels, and I need to adapt my lessons to these differences in my class. One thing is for sure: I know I always will try to be positive and see the good sides of children! (Burcin Bilgin, 2009)

Rest and regularity. Because many children grow up in an unstructured environment and parents often do not realize how hard school is for these children and let them go to bed late, they have moments of rest inserted in the program. This usually takes half an hour and then also put on soothing music. I am glad the teachers here take this into account, because young children need to learn a lot and that is just very tiring for them. You can also see that afterwards many children are more relaxed and more able to concentrate on their work. (Emmelie van Leeuwen, 2008)

Inspiring learning environment. The lecture that Earl Carter gave really stayed with me. Teaching urban students is like guiding students to follow the Yellow Brick Road in Wizard of Oz. Dorothy used the yellow brick road to get to Oz. The yellow brick road also represents real life. Every kid has a yellow brick road in his or her life or school career. For every kid that road is different. Some will make it all the way to college, others will drop out before they have reached high school. But the most important thing is that the teacher has an influence on that road. A teacher can make a difference for a kid on his or her path to success. It is the teacher who can motivate children and can let them learn in a way that is fun so they want to learn and think it is fun to go to school and make an effort. So the road a kid is walking is not the road that the kid will keep walking on. The road can become longer or shorter. I think it is important that you, as a teacher, make that road as long and as inspiring as possible. Every kid has the right to good education. To reach their dream, you have to know where their interests lie, what their strong skills are as well as their weak ones, without which, the children will not reach their dreams. Only you can make a difference! (Brenda Geestman, 2009)

To create a positive urban setting you should consider several points. You should provide a safe learning environment so each child will feel safe in every way, alone and together. In addition, it is an absolute must to base the relationship between teacher and children on trust. Make sure you know their background and look into the different cultures. At that time the child will feel more understood. Children will confide in the teacher slowly and that is important for the school progress of the child. It is important you are able to deal with your own position as a good teacher. You have enormous power and you should not abuse it. Structure in the classroom ensures that each child knows what to do. In my class, the teacher has prepared a calendar with different strips. These colorful strips all had meanings. The purple was, for example, "happy," and the blue was "sad" and so on. Every morning the children had to put the colored strip that applied to their state of mind next to their names. In that way you could see exactly how a child felt every day. (Pricilla de Korte, 2008)

Conclusion

The two weeks in America have had a major impact on students and lecturers. We were confronted with our own images of the United States, perceptions of American education, the expectations we had of the disadvantaged, and teaching at urban schools. Through numerous student questions, daily group discussions and school activities both students and instructors were able to critically reflect on our visions and attitudes.

Students concluded that education in urban schools in Philadelphia is characterized by providing well organized structures, raising high expectations, offering knowledge and keys from the start, role modeling for students from various ethnic backgrounds, paying attention to the work of the students, taking pride in student achievements, progress and products, and enhancing their self confidence. These themes are also extensively shared and highly valued in Dutch urban schools. The Philadelphia Urban Seminar was an impressive experience, which has enabled both students and instructors to affirm their educational values and reflect on urban issues in an international setting.

Reference

CBS (2009). Central Bureau of Statistics: http://www.cbs.nl/nlNL/menu/themas/bevolking/cijfers/extra/bevolkingsteller.htm, retrieved on September 1, 2009.

ETEN (2009). European Teacher Network: http://www.eten-online.org/, retrieved on October 26, 2009.

JOS (2009). Rotterdam Community on Education, Youth and Society. *Rotterdamse Onderwijsmonitor, primair en voortgezet onderwijs in Rotterdam.* JOS: Rotterdam.

University (2009). Rotterdam University Website: http://rotterdamuniversity.nl/, retrieved on October 26, 2009.

(G.R. Rodrigues and E. Fonville-kühlmann are instructors at the University of Rotterdam in Netherlands, Europe.)

Life of Urban Children: Struggle and Challenge
Nurun N. Begum

I traveled to the United States from Bangladesh, where I grew up in an urban setting. Most of the people in my country want to live in an urban setting because it is full of opportunities needed for a better life. This is not only true for Bangladesh, but also true for other Asian countries such as China and India. When I moved to the United States as a student, I reviewed a good amount of literature about urban students, urban life, and teaching in urban settings (Scott, 2003; Swartz, 2003; Melnick & Zeichne, 1998; Tatum, 1997; Zeichner & Melnick, 1996). Based on my research, I came to realize that most of the pre-service teachers are afraid to teach in urban settings. I was surprised, and at the same time was curious, to know about this fear. In the mean time, as a researcher, I got the opportunity to be involved in the Philadelphia Urban Seminar. As a part of my job, I reviewed the reflection papers written by the pre-service teachers who had participated in the Urban Seminar from 1997 to 2006. I also reviewed the pre- and post-questionnaire data which were administered during the Urban Seminar. The primary focus of this research was pre-service teachers' attitude towards the urban children, urban people, urban parents, urban teachers, urban administrators, urban school, urban life, and teaching in urban settings.

Although my research findings were interesting and eye opening, it did not give me enough information about the life of urban children. In the years of 2007 and 2008, I took my student teachers to Philadelphia to participate in the Urban Seminar. This gave me the opportunity to visit several school buildings and classrooms. I was fortunate to see those bright, brilliant, curious, eager to learn, innocent faces in the urban classrooms where stereotypical views labeled them as dumb, stupid or unruly kids.

I had a total of 16 student teachers who were placed in Kindergarten to fourth grade settings in different schools in north, northeast and northwest regions in Philadelphia. On the day that I was driving my student teachers from East Stroudsburg to Philadelphia, I observed the anxiety, fear, and shakiness among them. But at the end of the seminar, when I was driving back from Philadelphia to East Stroudsburg I observed the emotion and tears in my student teachers; I heard the stories of the children in their classrooms.

During the urban seminar, the student teachers had many small group meetings with their respective university faculty members. In those small group discussions, the student teachers shared the stories that they witnessed in their classrooms. They also described different stories on their reflection papers and journals. This paper is aimed at presenting those stories that were narrated by the student teachers as well as the faculty members during the Philadelphia Seminar.

Urban Children

Kids are kids no matter where they were born. Being Hispanic, Latino, Asian, European, or African is all about our skin color and appearance. In terms of our emotional, physical and cognitive development we all grow up in the same way. The society and the environment that we are in make a difference in our life. Tarnishing urban children as dumb, stupid, and unruly puts a label on the urban children. Most of the student teachers realized that news and media coverage has an influence on developing this kind of negative views about the urban children. One student teacher stated that "In news and media what we do not see or hear all the time is about the stories of bright, brilliant, smart children in urban settings." The society and environment also influence children to act in certain way. The student teacher shared a story of a boy, which illustrates the influence of the society and environment in a child's life. A nine-year old boy walked around and acted like he was a "thug" as he would call himself. The boy mentioned that his older brothers acted in a certain way, so he should too. He did not think he would make it through high school because he would be in jail or just drop out before graduation.

My student teachers have come across some children in their classrooms who love to learn, and want to come to school. This is because they realize that it is the only way those children are able to get some type of safe, warm, and welcoming environment. The student teachers also observed that some children in their class were very clingy, and constantly asking questions and telling them they loved them. It was because those children in their classroom did not get enough attention at home either because they were neglected or did not receive sufficient love or support from a parent or guardian. The student teachers also noticed that many urban children live in foster care, or come from broken families with either one or no parents. However, the one shock that one of the student teachers had to face was that some of the children in her class had not even reached the age of five when they became victims of sexual and physical abuse, and even worse, rape. Three of twenty eight children in her class reported that they had already been raped before the age of five. The student teacher stated "soon after, tears immediately came to my eyes as I glanced at the students. I could not believe that a child so young was sexually assaulted in ways that I cannot even bear to write about."

One of my student teachers shared a story about a boy whose father had been beating him with a belt. Throughout the year this boy's father would physically abuse the boy when the classroom teacher would send a sad face on his behavior chart. After a while, the teacher noticed that the young boy was coming to school with bruises and black eyes. After an investigation the teacher became aware of how his father abused him when he got a sad face on his behavior chart. From that point on the teacher never sent a sad face home with him again. Another incident was shared by a student teacher about a young girl who had witnessed something terrible happen to another family member. The girl took the student teacher aside, and asked whether the student teacher would help her to write a letter to her brother in the hospital. When the student wanted to know why the girl wanted to write the letter, the girl explained that her brother was setting up a drug deal, and in the mean time was shot in the face and chest by another man. The girl wanted to let her brother know how much she loved him. The student teacher stated "as much as I felt the pain and suffering for this little girl, the girl kept her head up and only considered positive thoughts about her brother's survival and being okay again." To reflect on the life of urban children, one student teacher wrote the following:

> I saw real life. I heard stories of eight and ten-year-old
> girls being pimped out by an uncle, I saw a bullet wound on
> a thirteen-year-old that shattered the left side of his hip, I
> talked to a boy whose twenty-year-old brother would be in
> jail for the next six years, and I felt the heartache that the
> students carried with them to school because they just lost
> a member of their family, church, or community. Those are
> the moments that I will remember the clearest.

Teachers in Urban Settings

The Urban Seminar participants shared a lot of positive and negative stories about the teachers in urban classrooms. One of my student teachers indicated that "my cooperating teacher completely changed my views on urban classroom; my cooperating teacher is a woman who has a heart of gold, and treats every single one of her students as if they were her own. Every single one of her students knew that they could go to her if they ever needed to vent or discuss their problems." Another student teacher mentioned that her cooperating teacher would never be able to work in a rural or suburban school because she would feel like she would not be able to face the normal way of life that rural and suburban kids are so generously given. The student teacher also mentioned that if her cooperating teacher has ever to leave the urban classroom, it would be like a prisoner being let go on parole after being in jail for so long. Another student teacher shared that, being a school principal for ten years in a rural school district setting, her cooperating teacher moved in Philadelphia as a teacher to make a difference in children's lives.

Some student teachers also have witnessed countless teachers who had given up on their students and would force the child to sit behind a desk without much care because the child became so undisciplined and out of control that there is nothing left for him/her to do. There was a situation described by a student teacher about a child named "Y." He lost his reading book and sat out during reading class everyday about a week because he did not have it. His father came into school one morning to discuss this situation with her cooperating teacher. The teacher informed the father that his son would get a new book when the old one would be paid for. The child's father did not send in the money for another two days, so the child sat out for another two days, even though the situation was not his fault. The student teacher stated "not only was the classroom teacher punishing the child by making him sit out, but she was also depriving the child of his education for over a week!"

Home Obligation

In an urban setting, often a child's life is very unclear. Children usually worry about their toys, books or cartoon characters. In the urban setting, however, the children's life is often totally different. They have to worry about food, clothes, home, safety and other obligations towards their families. Many children come from low income families and have many obligations that may take priority over school. It is hard to imagine that five to ten-year-old children have to cook dinner, give the little brother or sister a bath, and put him to bed all because his/her mother, the only working person in the house, is headed off to her second shift of the day. One student teacher shared a story about a child in her class who came to her during 100-book challenge time, which was silent reading time. The child asked her whether he could read to her. The child read one book to her. The student teacher appraised the child for having done an awesome job and tried to head towards another child; the boy pulled the student teacher back down and asked whether he could read another book to her because his parents at home never had time to listen to him read.

Summary

Many urban children are less fortunate because most of their school buildings are old and resources are scarce. Some school buildings do not have an adequate library or a computer lab, although the teachers are provided with many books and classrooms equipped with five computers. Our student teachers also noticed that the music teacher floats around from classroom to classroom because he does not have his own room. Urban children often go home, not able to access all the resources that a suburban child can. Poverty and different social barriers make the lives of many urban children really unfortunate.

In this article the stories are about life, suffering, and hope of urban children. These stories are real. Although the urban students are making a lot of stories every day, this paper only portrays those stories that motivated some pre-service teachers to change their attitude towards urban life and urban children. These stories have brought tears, given them pain and encouraged them to be strong and dedicated. From these stories, pre-service teachers developed their profound passion, professional commitment and career dedication, which are the foundation of their hope—hope for all urban children.

References

Melnick, S. L. & Zeichner, K. M. (1998). Teacher education's responsibility to address diversity issues: Enhancing institutional capacity: *Theory to Practice, 37(2),* 163-171.

Scott, R. M. (1995). Helping teacher education students develop positive attitudes towards ethnic minority. *Equality and Excellence in Education, 28(2),* 69-73.

Swartz, E. (2003). Teaching White pre-service teachers: Pedagogy for change. *Urban Education, 38*(3), 255–278.

Tatum, B. D. (1997). *Why are all the black kids sitting together in the cafeteria?* New York, NY: Basic Books.

Zeichner, K., & Melnick, S. (1996). The role of community field experiences in preparing teachers for cultural diversity. In K. Zeichner M.L Melnick & S. Gomez (Eds.), *Currents of reform in Pre-service Teacher Education*: (pp. 109–132) New York, NY: Teachers College Press.

(Nurun N. Begum is an assistant professor at East Stroudsburg University.)

Figure 6.2 Hope and action at Germantown Center

For Urban and All Students
Julie Q. Bao and George R. Bieger

The Philadelphia Urban Seminar reached a high point in 2009 with regard to numbers of participants, institutions, and facilitating schools. After that, national economic problems grew and began to affect every state, including Pennsylvania. With a looming budget deficit and a major change of leadership in the Pennsylvania State System of Higher Education (PASSHE), the Pennsylvania Academy for the Profession of Teaching and Learning (PAPTL) decided to cut its financial support to the Philadelphia Urban Seminar and started talking about more regionalized urban education programs. As a result, continuation of the Urban Seminar was in great jeopardy.

On July 8, 2009, Dr. Larry Vold of Indiana University of Pennsylvania (IUP) broke the sad news of the budget cut, by PASSHE, for the immensely popular Philadelphia Urban Seminar. He lamented in his email announcement to all coordinators that with all the wisdom of PASSHE's leadership, the administrators found the Urban Seminar expendable. Consequently, the financial support for the Urban Seminar of 2009–2010 academic year was not forthcoming. He further explained that due to failure to negotiate a contract that would allow him to have release time to coordinate the program, he had to resign from IUP. Dr. Vold, however, also sent a good wishes letter to all coordinators of the Urban Seminar, and expressed his determination to help explore all avenues to continue the program in creative ways.

Urban Seminars Are Not Expendable

When the news of PASSHE's budget cut and Dr. Vold' resignation reached the Urban Seminar coordinators on other campuses, professors responded unanimously: "No, the Urban Seminars are not expendable." Following are unsolicited testimonials quoted from communication messages among Urban Seminar coordinators.

Dr. Armitage of California University of PA wrote:

The students from California University of PA have consistently responded that the Philadelphia Seminar was one of the most powerful experiences of their college career. Most, if not all participants have said, "All education majors should have to take this course." Several of my students have, as a result of this experience, sought after urban teaching positions. I recently received an email from a former Philadelphia Urban Seminar student in which she informed me that she had just been offered a position in the Pittsburgh School District. She said, "I know that my experiences at Philadelphia helped me to get this teaching position."

Dr. Jenny of Slippery Rock University commented:

It came as quite a bombshell to read of Larry's resignation and the lack of regard that Indiana University of PA obviously holds for the Urban Seminar that Dr. Vold would not be allowed three credits of release time to continue to lead this most valuable program. As Ted Kennedy was to Health Care and Civil Rights, Dr. Vold has been the heart and driving force behind the Urban Seminar. This Seminar has been life changing for every student who has participated. Most of the PASSHE schools are in rural areas and consist of students who have had very little contact with other races. This Seminar has been vital in reshaping their narrow views into citizens of the world. The Seminar impacts 500 college students annually across the Commonwealth as they in turn impact the students in the inner-city schools in Philadelphia and their families. The Urban Seminar has a ripple effect on others that is immeasurable.

Dr. Rivera of Philadelphia Biblical University echoed:

When I became a professor at Philadelphia Biblical University, one of the first projects I worked on as Director of Student Teaching was getting connected to the Urban Seminar through Larry. In three short years, the participation of our students grew from 8 to 28. Of the students who participated in the Urban Seminar, several are now teaching in Philadelphia. Had it not been for the Urban Seminar, these students would not have considered becoming urban educators. Larry's vision and concern for staffing schools with dedicated and culturally equipped teachers is an achievement he can be proud of.

Dr. Hoover of Bloomsburg University wrote, "As is obvious, the Seminar has had a tremendous impact on both our students and on us. I know for certain that I have grown as a person and as a professor as a result of the program."

Dr. Johnson of Kutztown University said:

The news of the demise and I mean death of the Seminar has jettisoned me into a phase of mourning. It appears that things that really work and make strides to educate novice teachers about the realities of urban teaching have taken a back seat to the bureaucratic excuses once again. It will not take years but only moments for them to see what a foolish decision this is. What needs to happen is to mobilize testimony of the thousands of students who have been touched by this program... I have never met such committed, smart, giving, and truly loving individuals as Larry Vold, and everyone that I have worked with in the last nine years.

Dr. Colleen Poole at Cabrini College summed up the sentiments of the faculty group:

We teach all year and often wonder if we are making a difference, but during those two weeks in May we immediately know the answer! Having the opportunity to share the Urban Seminar with my students has been the most rewarding part of my teaching career. Watching the students grow as world citizens, in such a short time, is amazing and exciting. They challenge themselves to question who they are and what they really know and believe. The students, who have participated, from Cabrini College, return to campus wanting all education majors to be required to participate in the program. No other part of our teacher education program can match the impact that this experience offers regarding education, urban education, teaching strategies, classroom management, diversity and social justice.

Dr. McGinley of West Chester University (WCU) immediately started reexamining of her student data. She added: "WCU has been collecting, organizing, and analyzing our qualitative data over the years. I believe Colleen gets at our sentiments as a faculty member. To observe such great change of students so quickly is incredible."

Dr. Vagliardo of East Stroudsburg University stated:
East Stroudsburg University students who have participated in the Philadelphia Urban Seminar frequently refer to the experience as transformative. Like their counterparts from other PASSHE and private universities, the majority of the Seminar students are from suburban or rural environments, and have had limited experience in diverse, urban settings. The intense two weeks the students spend living and teaching in Philadelphia provides new awareness and understanding that far transcends the short time that they are in the city. For some, the experience

awakens new possibilities of teaching in an urban school. For many, it provides and develops an open mindedness and commitment to excellence for the increasingly diverse students they will teach. For all, the Urban Seminar provides an experience upon which to reflect as they learn and grow as beginning educators.

Dr. Melvin of Edinboro University had a campus computer system break down on the day that budget cut was announced. When the Edinboro's message system was back, she joined the discussion:

> ...I am just now getting this unfortunate and unbelievable news... We can only hope and pray that after reading the heartfelt responses, those in charge will realize the impact this will have on not only our university students, but also on those students in the Philadelphia School District.

In addition to voicing frustrations and disagreement over PASSHE's budget cut for the Urban Seminar, the faculty coordinators also took positive actions to enable the program to continue. Some wrote to the Dean of IUP, trying to avert the circumstance that led to Dr. Vold's resignation; Some wrote to PASSHE and other administrators to get clarifications. Many consulted or negotiated with their own college deans to find out the possibilities of carrying on the Urban Seminar on their own campus budget. All coordinators were hoping that the Urban Seminar would continue.

Preparations for Urban Seminar 2010

As a result of the concerted efforts of many coordinators, Dr. Vold announced on Oct. 19, 2009 that Philadelphia School District was willing to facilitate the Urban Seminar again. Within ten minutes of his email, faculty members from five universities committed their willingness for participation. Within twenty-four hours, ten university coordinators joined the committed group. Some, however, had to eventually back out of their commitment due to circumstances of their home campus.

Despite faculty's frustration over PASSHE's budget cut and unclear financial pictures on their own campus, their preparation for Urban Seminar 2010 never stopped. After Dr. Vold's resignation, the urban coordinators on the IUP campus continued the fight under the leadership of Drs. Monte Tidwell and George Bieger, who also gained support from the Department of Professional Studies in Education. Moreover, faculty coordinators from all campuses involved kept frequent correspondence to support each other. Dr. Jenny told IUP professors to "Keep the faith, Monte. We are behind you all the way and appreciate your efforts as well as George's to keep the program alive and thriving!" Deeply touched by the support of faculty from other campuses, Dr. Tidwell replied on behalf of Dr. Bieger and himself:

> Thanks to all of you for showing your strong support for Larry and for the Urban Seminar. George and I have already written a letter to the Dean that is signed by the majority of faculty in our department. I am attaching a copy for you to see. George also wrote a strong letter that has gone to our President and Provost. We are not giving up. I am meeting with the Dean this afternoon and will push for the release time necessary to coordinate the seminar…We have something special that greatly benefits our students. We will keep you posted as to what is happening on our end. Meanwhile, we are planning to recruit and we will be open with the students about the difficulties we are facing. Stay tuned and stay in touch.

When universities stopped sending coordinators to the preparation meetings at Harrisburg, faculty explored other possible meeting locations. Some professors suggested that coordinators use the National Association of Multicultural Education conference (to be held in PA) as a venue to continue their planning for Urban Seminar 2010.

Thanks to the great efforts of many facilitators the Philadelphia Urban Seminar took place again in May of 2010. There were 350 pre-service teachers from 13 universities who were placed in over 50 schools in the School District of Philadelphia. While the number is fewer than the previous year it is a significant number of participants, especially considering that students had to pay the full cost of the program since PASSHE's support had been eliminated. The success of the program without extra state or school district funding is a testimony to the campus coordinators and faculty, who, because of their commitment to the preparation of urban teachers, overcame opposition to the program and delivered a quality immersion experience. It is also a testament to both the pre-service teachers themselves who were willing to go the extra mile to become better teachers, and the mentor teachers in the Philadelphia public schools who served as excellent role models. At the completion of the manuscript, the preparations for Urban Seminar 2011 are still going on in multiple institutions.

Summary of the Urban Seminar

The Philadelphia Urban Seminar is a profound educational initiative in urban teacher training in America, which is created and executed by educators who are dedicated to urban teaching and learning. The program's continued success for the last 18 years has demonstrated vision, commitment, passion, and efforts of the facilitators involved. This program is characterized by its research base, inner-city immersion, a long term and massive operation, multi-faceted collaborations, and assessment of learning outcome. The following model highlights these five characteristics of the Urban Seminar:

Five Characteristics of the Philadelphia Urban Seminar

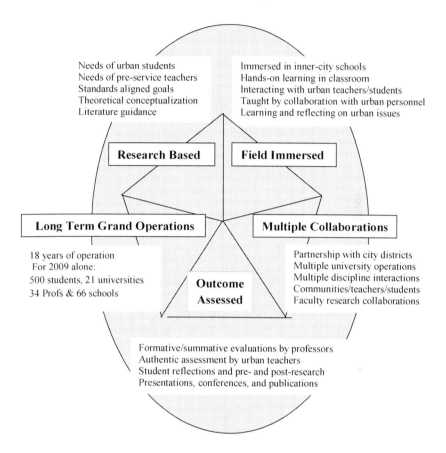

Figure 6.3 Five Characteristics of the Philadelphia Urban Seminar

The above Urban Seminar model illustrates that the Urban Seminar is research based. Multiple studies quoted in Chapter Five have indicated the urgent needs of urban students as well as those of pre-service teachers who need to know how to work with urban students, align state standards with urban classroom instruction, and how to teach urban students with culturally sensitive strategies. Based on these needs, the Urban Seminar Coordinating Committee devises pertinent learning goals and develops authentic learning tasks.

To accomplish these standards aligned learning goals, the Urban Seminar employs a total urban immersion approach, which grounds its participants firmly in the inner-city environment and provides pre-service teachers with a variety of hands-on urban teaching and learning experiences, such as requiring teacher candidates to attend professional development sessions and teaming them up with urban colleagues to learn how to manage urban classrooms. Additionally, it facilitates pre-service teachers to work with communities to put urban issues in perspective, and prepares them to seek job opportunities to teach urban students.

Moreover, Philadelphia Urban Seminar stands out on its program scope, length, and depth. Eighteen years of urban immersion is a tremendous human endeavor that demands incredible commitment on its participants and facilitators. With the 2009 group of over 500 teacher candidates and 34 professors from 21 universities staying in student dorms for two weeks and, at the same time, working with 66 schools and multiple community centers, it is one of the largest and longest urban immersion teacher training programs in inner-cities of America.

Furthermore, the Urban Seminar boasts exceptional collaboration and passion among its faculty coordinators and other facilitators. The collaboration ranges from university with districts to university with communities; from supervisors with cooperating teachers to professors with students. The Urban Education Conferences and Books mentioned in earlier articles are just a few of numerous collaboration examples. In addition, the passion demonstrated by participants in the program is remarkable. The program was supported by PASSHE for many years, which subsidized students' lodging while they paid regular tuition to take the course. Nevertheless, PASSHE's support waxed and waned depending on who was in charge of the Office, but for all the past 18 years, the faculty coordinators' passion for the urban cause and students has never diminished, which, to a great extent, underscores and sustains the success of the program.

Finally, the learning impact of the Urban Seminar was strongly supported by a plethora of quantitative and qualitative research. Apart from student and faculty testimonials the effectiveness of the program is corroborated by a nine-year longitudinal study, several doctoral dissertations, a few case studies and multiple qualitative research analyses. As a matter of fact, the whole book is a testimonial of the impact of the program. It is the multitude of research on student learning outcome that validates most the effectiveness of the Urban Seminar, and consequently places it among the most effective urban teacher training initiatives in American education.

By the end of 2009–2010 academic year, a generation of passionate Urban Seminar coordinators had retired, and some will soon retire, from this program. Though the program carried on in 2010 and the preparations for the 2011 Urban Seminar are still going on, it is difficult to change the fact that the scope of the Urban Seminar has been substantially reduced. This reduction is mainly due to PASSHE's budget cut in 2010, but it is also because of the vision, commitment, passion and the program priority of PASSHE in relation to urban education. Nevertheless, we believe this and more urban teacher training programs will continue in Pennsylvania and the nation. Those new programs might not be named as Urban Seminar; they might emerge in different cities with various scales and strategies, and they might be lead by different systems of education, but they will continue because preparing teachers that will be able to teach urban students is one of the most urgent needs in American education. The availability of qualified urban teachers is among the major factors that will decide on the future success of urban students.

In this book, we have presented some poignant stories along with our exciting learning experiences about the Philadelphia Urban Seminar to the public. We encourage all readers to reflect on these urban education issues in conjunction with their root causes and ramifications. To show respect for all efforts we observed to improve inner-city schools, we dedicate this book to students and educators who are striving to advance the urban learning conditions in America. As faculty coordinators of the Urban Seminar, we treasure this extraordinary learning experience dearly, and want to document this unique program for our current and future educators. We believe that together we have created a highly effective urban teacher training program, carried it out passionately, grown with students in it, and most importantly, in executing the Philadelphia Urban Seminar and helping urban and all students, we have jointly and ardently walked our talk in our teacher training profession for the last 18 years.

(Julie Q. Bao is a professor at Shippensburg University; George R. Bieger is a professor at Indiana University of PA.)

Appendix A. Urban Seminar Participating Universities

Bloomsburg University
California University
Cheyney University
Clarion University
Cabrini College
East Stroudsburg University
Edinboro University
Indiana University of PA
Juniata College
Kutztown University
Lock Haven University
Mansfield University
Millersville University
Robert Morris University
Rotterdam University, The Netherlands
Pennsylvania State University
Philadelphia Biblical University
Shippensburg University
Slippery Rock University
West Chester University
West Liberty University

Appendix B. Figure Captions

Chapter One
Figure 1.1 Go to school in the morning
Figure 1.2 Attending workshops after school
Figure 1.3 Visiting Norris Square Community Center
Chapter Five
Figure 5.1 Demographics of the sample
Figure 5.2 Comparison of concerns pre- and post- experience
Figure 5.3 Urban Seminar students at the Conference
Figure 5.4 Professors from 20 universities meeting at Philadelphia
Chapter Six
Figure 6.1 Reading at Norris Square Children's Festival
Figure 6.2 Hope and action at Germantown Center
Figure 6.3 Five Characteristics of the Philadelphia Urban Seminar
Back Cover Photo Captions (from top to bottom)
Figure 1 Learning hands-on math in classroom
Figure 2 Reporting to school
Figure 3 Finding our schools in Philadelphia
Figure 4 Visiting Norris Square Community Center
Figure 5 Mural Research in Philadelphia
Figure 6 Hope and action at Germantown Center
(All photos are taken by Julie Bao.)